Letts

KS2 Success

Age 7-11

Maths

Practice Workbook

Shaun Stirling

Numbers

Calculations

Fraction, Decimals and Percentages

Ratio and Proportion

Place value

1 Write the value of each red digit.

a. 467 .... **(1 mark)**   **b.** 783 .... **(1 mark)**

c. 359 .... **(1 mark)**   **d.** 4358 .... **(1 mark)**

e. 6783 .... **(1 mark)**   **f.** 14338 .... **(1 mark)**

g. 32214 .... **(1 mark)**   **h.** 345271 .... **(1 mark)**

2 Look at these digits.

a. Using all of the cards, what is the largest number you can make?

(1 mark)

....

b. Using all of the cards, what is the smallest number you can make?

(1 mark)

....

Ordering numbers

1 Order these numbers from smallest to largest:

a. 212   2120   2021   221   12120   21210   **(1 mark)**

................, ..., ..., ..., ..., ...

b. 667   6607   6670   766   66707   67706   **(1 mark)**

................, ..., ..., ..., ..., ...

2 Order these numbers from largest to smallest:

a. 31313   33311   3113   3311   313   331   **(1 mark)**

................, ..., ..., ..., ..., ...

b. 449   949   14494   14994   1499   1944   **(1 mark)**

................, ..., ..., ..., ..., ...

Greater than and less than

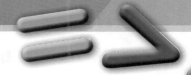

1 Put either **<** or **>** between these pairs of numbers to make each statement correct.

a. 4600 ☐ 4060   **(1 mark)**   **b.** 10 033 ☐ 10 303   **(1 mark)**

c. 12 269 ☐ 12 469   **(1 mark)**   **d.** 423 486 ☐ 432 008   **(1 mark)**

2 Put the symbol **=**, **<** or **>** between each pair of operations to make each statement correct.

a. 120 + 60 ☐ 200 − 20   **(1 mark)**   **b.** 350 + 60 ☐ 700 − 360   **(1 mark)**

c. 1200 − 300 ☐ 10 × 80   **(1 mark)**   **d.** 0.9 + 0.2 ☐ 4.8 ÷ 4   **(1 mark)**

Numbers in words

1 Write these numbers in words.

a. 12 405 .... **(1 mark)**

....

b. 8 402 798 .... **(1 mark)**

....

c. 312 009 .... **(1 mark)**

....

2 Write these numbers in digits.

a. Twenty-eight thousand, six hundred and two   **(1 mark)**

....

b. Six hundred and two thousand, seven hundred and thirty-six   **(1 mark)**

....

c. One million, five hundred and eleven   **(1 mark)**

....

Total $\frac{}{28}$

Rounding numbers

1 Round these numbers to the nearest **10**.

   a. 67 ....   **(1 mark)**

   b. 83 ....   **(1 mark)**

   c. 95 ....   **(1 mark)**

   d. 19 896 ....   **(1 mark)**

2 Round these numbers to the nearest **hundred**.

   a. 682 ....   **(1 mark)**

   b. 408 ....   **(1 mark)**

   c. 1970 ....   **(1 mark)**

   d. 56 911 ....   **(1 mark)**

3 Round these numbers to the nearest **thousand**.

   a. 1245 ....   **(1 mark)**

   b. 32 356 ....   **(1 mark)**

   c. 129 983 ....   **(1 mark)**

   d. 1 340 400 ....   **(1 mark)**

4 Seventy-four thousand, eight hundred and ninety-two people visited a museum. What is this rounded to the nearest:

   a. ten? ....   **(1 mark)**

   b. hundred? ....   **(1 mark)**

   c. thousand? ....   **(1 mark)**

Rounding money

1 Round these amounts of money to the nearest pound.

   a. £33.99 ....   **(1 mark)**

   b. £1.19 ....   **(1 mark)**

c. £1 639.52 ....   **(1 mark)**

d. £8.75 ....   **(1 mark)**

2 Dylan wants to buy a jacket that costs £34.99, a pair of trousers that cost £26.99 and a pair of trainers that cost £44.99.

Round each price to the nearest pound then find the approximate total.   **(2 marks)**

Show your working

Negative numbers

1 Calculate:

a. $-5 + 14 =$ ....   **(1 mark)**

b. $-11 - 20 =$ ....   **(1 mark)**

c. $-17 + 30 =$ ....   **(1 mark)**

d. $15 - 19 =$ ....   **(1 mark)**

2 The temperature in a kitchen freezer is −17°C. In the kitchen the temperature is 15°C. What is the difference in temperature between the two?   **(1 mark)**

....

3 Jet had £46.00 in the bank, but he spent £50.00. What is the balance of his bank account?   **(1 mark)**

....

Total $\dfrac{}{27}$

BIDMAS

① Calculate:

a. $\dfrac{(14 - 2)}{4}$ = ... **(1 mark)**

b. $10^2 - (4 \times 6) + 45$ = ... **(1 mark)**

c. $4 + 5^2 - 6 \times 4$ = ... **(1 mark)**

d. $(1225 + 2775) + 2000 \div 5$ = ... **(1 mark)**

② Which one of these operations will have the greatest total? Explain your answer. **(2 marks)**

A: $(6 \times 4.5) + 5.5 - 3$ = ?

B: $6 \times (4.5 + 5.5) - 3$ = ?

....

Top tip!

Remember that BIDMAS stands for Brackets, Indices, Division, Multiplication, Addition and Subtraction – the order that you complete these operations.

Missing symbol

① Write the correct sign, **=**, **<** or **>** into these statements to make them correct.

a. $(8 \div 4) - 2$ ☐ $8 \div (4 - 2)$ **(1 mark)**

b. $(7 + 6) - 4$ ☐ $7 + (6 - 4)$ **(1 mark)**

c. $(3 \times 15) - 8$ ☐ $3 \times (15 - 8)$ **(1 mark)**

d. $100 \div 10^2 \times 1000$ ☐ $\sqrt{100} \div 10 \times 1000$ **(1 mark)**

Missing numbers

1 What numbers are missing from these equations?

a. $2 \times 130 - \boxed{} = 50 \times 3 + 70$ **(1 mark)**

b. $3^2 \times 5 - 7 = 4^2 \times 2 + \boxed{}$ **(1 mark)**

c. $(\boxed{} \times 4) - 37 = 5^2 + 2 \times 9$ **(1 mark)**

2 Choose two numbers that would make these equations correct.

a. $(5 \times \boxed{}) + \boxed{} = 120$ **(1 mark)**

b. $6^2 - 12 = \boxed{} \times \boxed{} + 4$ **(1 mark)**

Missing brackets

1 Insert a **pair of brackets** to make each equation correct.

a. $52 - 3 \div 7 = 42 \div 6$ **(1 mark)**

b. $225 \div 5 = 3 + 2 \times 9$ **(1 mark)**

c. $2 + 3 \times 4 + 5 \times 6 = 50$ **(1 mark)**

d. $7 + 6 \times 5 + 4 = \dfrac{122}{2}$ **(1 mark)**

Multiples

1 Circle all the multiples of nine in this list. **(1 mark)**

89, 108, 120, 126, 138

2 Circle all the multiples of six in this list. **(1 mark)**

72, 603, 702, 716, 8022

3 Which of these numbers is **not** a multiple of 50? **(1 mark)**

1050, 5000, 5005, 10000, 50000

....

4 What number is the largest two-digit multiple of four and of six? **(1 mark)**

....

5 What number is the smallest three-digit multiple of five and eight?

(1 mark)

....

6 Louis says, "I added a multiple of four to a multiple of three and made 60."
What two numbers might Louis have used? **(1 mark)**

....

7 Complete this sentence. **(1 mark)**

All multiples of eight are also multiples of ☐ and ☐ .

8 Miller says, "Whenever I multiply two multiples of three together,
I get a multiple of six."
Is she correct?

Yes ☐   No ☐

Explain how you know. **(1 mark)**

....

....

Factors

1 Look at this Venn diagram.

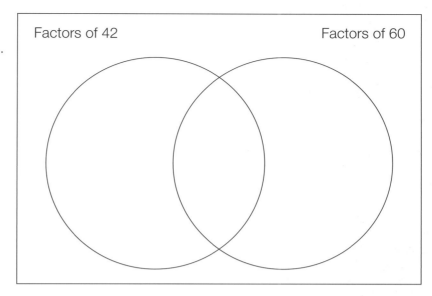

Factors of 42   Factors of 60

a. Write these numbers into the correct sectors of the diagram.

(2 marks)

b. What are the common factors of 42 and 60? .... **(1 mark)**

c. What is the highest common factor of 42 and 60? .... **(1 mark)**

2 16 and 25 have an odd number of factors. Write down another number that has an odd number of factors. **(1 mark)**

....

3 What is the total of all the factors of 15? .... **(1 mark)**

4 Idris thought of two prime numbers.
He says, "The difference between my two numbers is four and their total is 42."
What are Idris' two numbers? **(1 mark)**

....

5 Write all the factors of 26 that are also factors of 52. **(1 mark)**

....

6 Complete these equations with prime numbers.

a. ☐ × ☐ = 35   **b.** ☐ × ☐ = 39 **(2 marks)**

Total ___
18

Addition with whole numbers

1 Calculate:

a. 25 + 79 = ... **(1 mark)**

b. 101 + 70 = ... **(1 mark)**

c. 249 + 251 + 250 = ... **(1 mark)**

d. 6006 + 4004 + 34 = ... **(1 mark)**

2 Complete: **(4 marks)**

a.
$$\begin{array}{r} 2376 \\ +\ \ 523 \\ \hline \end{array}$$

b.
$$\begin{array}{r} 2329 \\ + 6145 \\ \hline \end{array}$$

c.
$$\begin{array}{r} 7088 \\ + 4777 \\ \hline \end{array}$$

d.
$$\begin{array}{r} 67\,409 \\ +\ \ \ \ 898 \\ 439 \\ \hline \end{array}$$

Addition with decimals

1 Calculate:

a. 1.5 + 2.5 = ... **(1 mark)**

b. 25.6 + 12 + 15.4 = ... **(1 mark)**

c. 3.07 + 1.03 + 0.2 = ... **(1 mark)**

d. £2.25 + £3.25 + £6.50 = ... **(1 mark)**

2 Complete: **(4 marks)**

a.
$$\begin{array}{r} £200.67 \\ + £105.99 \\ \hline \end{array}$$

b.
$$\begin{array}{r} 46.06\ m \\ + 00.59\ m \\ \hline \end{array}$$

c.
$$\begin{array}{r} 1.5\ litres \\ + 0.330\ litres \\ \hline \end{array}$$

d.
$$\begin{array}{r} 99.071 \\ + 10.489 \\ 83.001 \\ \hline \end{array}$$

Solving problems

1 **a.** Write the smallest whole number to make this correct. 63 + ☐ > 84 **(1 mark)**

b. Write the greatest whole number to make this correct. 79 + ☐ < 93 **(1 mark)**

2 At half-term, Tanya first goes to visit her grandparents' house. The journey is 234 miles each way. She comes home before going to visit her cousin who lives 56 miles away. She then returns home again.
How far does she travel in total? **(1 mark)**

....

....

3 Ali is making some bedroom curtains. She needs to make four curtains and each curtain has to be 1.2 m wide.
What is their total width? **(1 mark)**

....

....

4 Isla buys tickets for two concerts. Together they cost £49. One ticket cost £15 more than the other one.
How much did each ticket cost? **(1 mark)**

....

....

5 Three brothers get pocket money. Andrew gets £1.25 more than Alex. Aidan gets £5.50. Alex gets £1.50 less than Aidan.
How much pocket money do they get altogether? **(1 mark)**

....

....

Top tip!

When adding numbers, look for pairs of numbers that make 10 or 100. Watch out for doubles or near doubles, for example 24 and 26.

Total — 22

Small differences

1 Calculate the differences between these amounts.

a. 2003 – 1998 = ... **(1 mark)**

b. 1006 cm – 993 cm = ... **(1 mark)**

c. 10 001 – 9985 = ... **(1 mark)**

d. £20.05 – £19.99 = ... **(1 mark)**

Subtraction with whole numbers

1 Complete: **(4 marks)**

a.
```
  2941
−  731
_____
```

b.
```
  5075
−   46
_____
```

c.
```
  9120
− 2566
_____
```

d.
```
  5031
−  426
_____
```

Subtraction with decimals

1 Calculate:

a. 10.5 – 8.5 = ... **(1 mark)**

b. 60.3 – 50.9 = ... **(1 mark)**

c. £125.89 – £34.90 = ... **(1 mark)**

d. 0.8 cm – 0.75 cm = ... **(1 mark)**

2 Complete: **(4 marks)**

a.
```
  2.456
− 0.237
_____
```

b.
```
  £92.30
− £70.35
_____
```

c.
```
  4.910
− 0.707
_____
```

d.
```
  119.1
−  6.456
_____
```

Solving problems

Top tip! Although you should be familiar with column subtraction, when finding the differences between numbers and amounts that are close together, it's quicker to count up from the smaller to the larger amount.

❶ Berlin is 577.8 miles from London. Amsterdam is 222.16 miles from London. How many miles nearer to London is Amsterdam than Berlin?

(1 mark)

....

....

❷ Ava has £10.00. She buys two books that cost £3.95 and £2.95. How much does she have left?

(1 mark)

....

....

❸ Simon runs 200 m in 39.42 seconds. Kian runs the same distance in 26.95 seconds. How many seconds faster than Simon is Kian?

(1 mark)

....

....

❹ Two friends share a 1.5 litre bottle of lemonade. One pours a glass of 350 ml. The other pours a glass of 250 ml. How much lemonade is left in the bottle?

(1 mark)

....

....

❺ Sohail and Karl both buy a milkshake. Sohail pays with a five pound note and receives £2.25 change. Karl pays with a ten pound note and receives £6.85 change. How much more did Karl's milkshake cost?

(1 mark)

....

....

❻ Iona had a length of ribbon. She cut off 30 cm and gave what she had left to Niamh. Niamh cut off 20 cm, then gave half of what she had left to Bella. Bella received 40 cm of ribbon. What length of ribbon did Iona have?

(1 mark)

....

....

Total $\frac{}{22}$

Grid method

1 Use the grids to complete these multiplications.

a. 435 × 44 = ... **(1 mark)**

	400	30	5
40			
4			

b. 629 × 72 = ... **(1 mark)**

	600	20	9
70			
2			

c. 818 × 48 = ... **(1 mark)**

	800	10	8
40			
8			

d. 1234 × 346 = ... **(1 mark)**

	1000	200	30	4	
					300
					40
					6

Short multiplication

1 Complete: **(4 marks)**

a.
```
  435
×   7
─────
```

b.
```
  287
×   4
─────
```

c.
```
 6175
×   6
─────
```

d.
```
 8306
×   9
─────
```

Long multiplication

1 Complete: **(4 marks)**

   a.   301   **b.**   654   **c.**   807   **d.**   2397
        ×   32   ×   46   ×   94   ×   15

        _____   _____   _____   _____

Solving problems

1 Ailsa and 14 friends go out for a birthday meal. The price per head is £16.
What is the total cost?   **(1 mark)**

....

2 **a.** Joe has 35 boxes of power balls to sell at the school fair. Each box contains 20 balls.
How many balls does Joe have to sell?   **(1 mark)**

....

   b. If Joe sells every ball for 25p, how much will he make?   **(1 mark)**

....

....

....

3 There are 24 children in Mrs Jones's class. For Forest School she needs to buy them all
waterproof coats and trousers. Coats cost £12.75 and trousers cost £9.55. How much
money will Mrs Jones need to equip her class?   **(1 mark)**

....

....

4 Olivia earns £5.50 an hour babysitting. In December she babysat for six hours a night
for nine nights. How much money did she earn?   **(1 mark)**

....

5 In this pyramid, each number is the product of the two numbers below it. Write the
missing numbers on the empty blocks.   **(1 mark)**

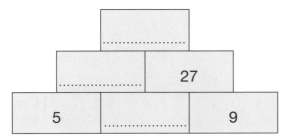

Total — 18

Short division

❶ Complete the following divisions.

a. $3\overline{)693}$ (1 mark)

b. $4\overline{)432}$ (1 mark)

c. $5\overline{)3575}$ (1 mark)

d. $9\overline{)8172}$ (1 mark)

Long division

❶ Complete the following divisions.

a. $15\overline{)555}$ (1 mark)

b. $24\overline{)528}$ (1 mark)

c. $48\overline{)9312}$ (1 mark)

d. $42\overline{)2730}$ (1 mark)

Remainders

❶ Complete these divisions and give any remainder as a fraction.

a. $4\overline{)531}$ (1 mark)

b. $6\overline{)1907}$ (1 mark)

❷ Complete these divisions and give any remainder as a decimal.

a. $25\overline{)360}$ (1 mark)

b. $16\overline{)8884}$ (1 mark)

Problem solving

1 Lyla is making party bags. She has 112 sweets to put into eight bags.
How many sweets can she put into each bag? **(1 mark)**

....

....

2 Seventy children arrive at a hostel on a school residential. Each dormitory
has eight beds.
How many dormitories will they need? **(1 mark)**

....

....

3 Jake has 456 football cards. He puts them into bundles of 12 to sell to
his friends.
How many bundles can he make? **(1 mark)**

....

....

4 A builder needs 5560 bricks to build an extension to a house.

a. The bricks are sold in pallets of 400. How many pallets will he need
to order? **(1 mark)**

....

....

b. Each pallet costs £280. What will the total cost be? **(1 mark)**

....

....

Total — 17

Multi-step problems

1 Ellie, Alex and Belinda take part in a charity walk.

- Ellie collects £18
- Alex collects £4.75 **more** than Belinda.
- Alex collects £7 **less** than Ellie.

Altogether how much money do the three children collect?   **(2 marks)**

....

....

2 Ruby buys two pairs of ballet shoes and a pair of tap shoes.
How much change does she get from £40?   **(2 marks)**

Ballet store prices

Tap shoes	£18.95
Jazz shoes	£15.50
Ballet shoes	£6.99

....

....

3 A meat samosa costs 30p more than a vegetarian samosa.
Mina bought a meat samosa and two vegetarian samosas for £1.80

How much does a vegetarian samosa cost?   **(2 marks)**

....

....

4 Isla visits the ice rink three times in a week.
She pays £6.50 per visit.

    a. A weekly saver pass costs £14
       How much would Isla have saved if she had bought a weekly pass? **(2 marks)**

....

....

    b. If Isla buys a £14 weekly saver pass for next week and uses it four times, what will
       the average cost of a trip be? **(2 marks)**

....

....

5 Emily is selling 200 baked potatoes.

- She sells 60 baked potatoes with cheese.
- She sells 25 baked potatoes with tuna.
- She sells twice as many with butter than with tuna.

How many does she sell with beans? **(2 marks)**

Menu
Baked potato with cheese
Baked potato with butter
Baked potato with beans
Baked potato with tuna

....

....

6 **a.** Alfie sells tickets for scout camp. He sells 230 tickets at £2.50 each.
      How much does he earn? **(1 mark)**

....

....

    b. Alfie buys sachets of hot chocolate. There are six sachets in a box. A group of
      eighty boys and girls and eight leaders are attending the scout camp.
      How many boxes of hot chocolate will he need to buy if they each have one drink
      of hot chocolate? **(1 mark)**

....

....

Total $\frac{}{14}$

Addition, subtraction, multiplication and division

1 456 + 567 =

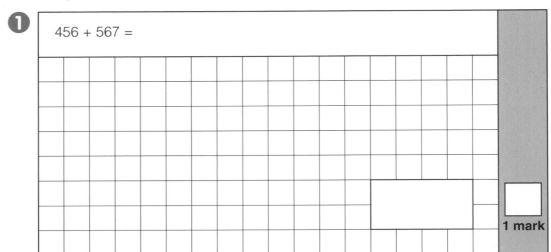

1 mark

2 134.67 + 8.685 =

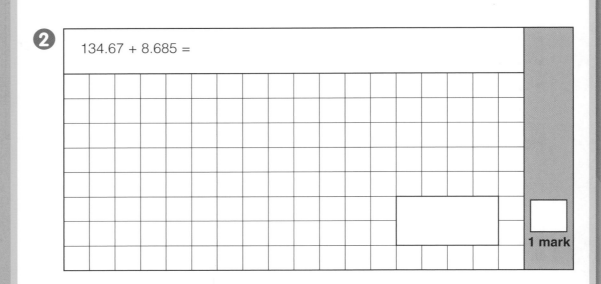

1 mark

3 1043 – 788 =

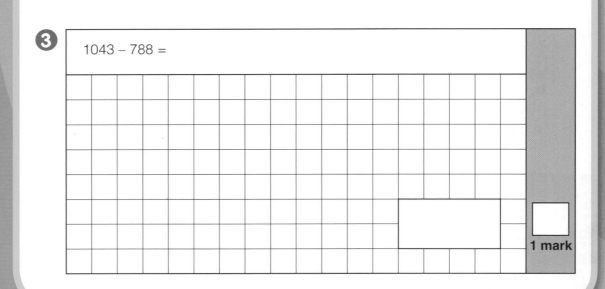

1 mark

4

5.6 × 20 =

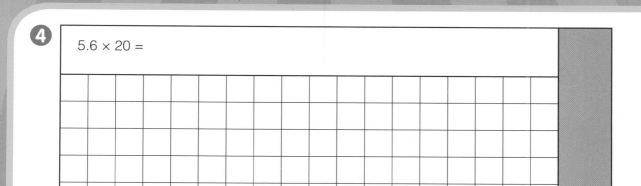

1 mark

5

1592 ÷ 4 =

1 mark

6

18.63 ÷ 9 =

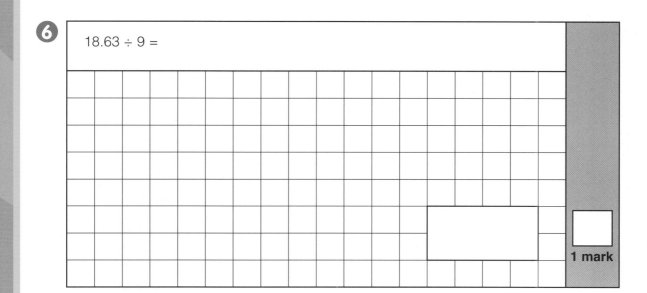

1 mark

Total — 6

Multiplication grids

1 Multiply the numbers together and write the answers into the grid.
How many you can complete in one minute? **(2 marks)**

×	8	3	9	5	10	12
4						
11						
6						
7						
2						

2 Fill in the missing numbers in these grids. **(3 marks)**

a.

×	7	....	....
2	14	16	18
....	21	....	....
....	....	32	36

b.

×	5	7	....
....	10	....	18
....	....	....	36
6	30	42	....

c.

×	11	....	....
9	99	108	....
....	88	96	80
....	77	84	....

Time yourself

3 Try to answer 60 questions in two minutes.

(4 marks)

1 7 × 3 = ...   **2** 1 × 11 = ...   **3** 2 × 6 = ...   **4** 11 × 4 = ...

5 5 × 6 = ...   **6** 2 × 8 = ...   **7** 3 × 2 = ...   **8** 9 × 10 = ...

9 8 × 4 = ...   **10** 11 × 2 = ...   **11** 11 × 9 = ...   **12** 11 × 8 = ...

13 8 × 10 = ...   **14** 6 × 9 = ...   **15** 8 × 11 = ...   **16** 5 × 11 = ...

17 2 × 8 = ...   **18** 7 × 4 = ...   **19** 8 × 8 = ...   **20** 6 × 11 = ...

21 12 × 10 = ...   **22** 6 × 1 = ...   **23** 2 × 3 = ...   **24** 10 × 7 = ...

25 6 × 12 = ...   **26** 10 × 6 = ...   **27** 4 × 10 = ...   **28** 9 × 6 = ...

29 6 × 2 = ...   **30** 4 × 9 = ...   **31** 11 × 3 = ...   **32** 11 × 7 = ...

33 10 × 12 = ...   **34** 4 × 6 = ...   **35** 9 × 4 = ...   **36** 8 × 7 = ...

37 3 × 4 = ...   **38** 9 × 4 = ...   **39** 6 × 8 = ...   **40** 4 × 2 = ...

41 12 × 9 = ...   **42** 11 × 12 = ...   **43** 2 × 10 = ...   **44** 7 × 1 = ...

45 5 × 9 = ...   **46** 8 × 9 = ...   **47** 9 × 5 = ...   **48** 7 × 6 = ...

49 4 × 5 = ...   **50** 7 × 12 = ...   **51** 8 × 12 = ...   **52** 7 × 8 = ...

53 2 × 11 = ...   **54** 4 × 10 = ...   **55** 10 × 9 = ...   **56** 9 × 6 = ...

57 9 × 11 = ...   **58** 3 × 4 = ...   **59** 10 × 1 = ...   **60** 2 × 12 = ...

Total — 9

Equivalent fractions

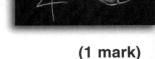

1 Complete to make these fractions equivalent.

a. $\dfrac{1}{3} = \dfrac{\boxed{}}{6}$ **(1 mark)**

b. $\dfrac{2}{4} = \dfrac{\boxed{}}{2}$ **(1 mark)**

c. $\dfrac{4}{5} = \dfrac{\boxed{}}{10}$ **(1 mark)**

d. $\dfrac{3}{12} = \dfrac{\boxed{}}{4}$ **(1 mark)**

e. $\dfrac{16}{24} = \dfrac{\boxed{}}{3}$ **(1 mark)**

f. $\dfrac{9}{15} = \dfrac{\boxed{}}{5}$ **(1 mark)**

2 Complete these rows of equivalent fractions.

a. $\dfrac{1}{4} = \dfrac{\boxed{}}{12} = \dfrac{6}{\boxed{}} = \dfrac{\boxed{}}{48}$ **(1 mark)**

b. $\dfrac{1}{3} = \dfrac{2}{\boxed{}} = \dfrac{4}{\boxed{}} = \dfrac{8}{\boxed{}}$ **(1 mark)**

3 Circle the fraction that is **not** equivalent.

a. $\dfrac{20}{100}$ $\dfrac{12}{50}$ $\dfrac{6}{25}$ $\dfrac{36}{150}$ **(1 mark)**

b. $\dfrac{6}{9}$ $\dfrac{36}{54}$ $\dfrac{30}{42}$ $\dfrac{20}{30}$ **(1 mark)**

Reducing fractions

1 Reduce these fractions to their simplest terms.

a. $\dfrac{10}{16} =$ ....   **(1 mark)**

b. $\dfrac{9}{12} =$ ....   **(1 mark)**

c. $\frac{18}{24}$ = ... **(1 mark)**

d. $\frac{15}{25}$ = ... **(1 mark)**

Mixed numbers and improper fractions

1 Convert these improper fractions to mixed numbers.

a. $\frac{27}{5}$ = ... **(1 mark)**

b. $\frac{43}{6}$ = ... **(1 mark)**

c. $\frac{56}{9}$ = ... **(1 mark)**

d. $\frac{71}{8}$ = ... **(1 mark)**

2 Convert these mixed numbers to improper fractions.

a. $4\frac{3}{4}$ = ... **(1 mark)**

b. $8\frac{6}{7}$ = ... **(1 mark)**

c. $10\frac{1}{10}$ = ... **(1 mark)**

d. $7\frac{2}{3}$ = ... **(1 mark)**

3 Insert the symbol **=**, **>** or **<** to make these statements correct.

a. $\frac{18}{5}$ ☐ $3\frac{3}{5}$ **(1 mark)**

b. $6\frac{3}{7}$ ☐ $\frac{43}{7}$ **(1 mark)**

c. $\frac{405}{100}$ ☐ $3\frac{90}{100}$ **(1 mark)**

d. $7\frac{2}{9}$ ☐ $\frac{65}{9}$ **(1 mark)**

Total $\overline{26}$

Ordering fractions

1 Write these fractions in order of size, smallest first.

a. $\dfrac{1}{2}$ $\dfrac{1}{3}$ $\dfrac{5}{6}$ $\dfrac{7}{12}$ **(1 mark)**

....

b. $\dfrac{4}{8}$ $\dfrac{3}{4}$ $\dfrac{10}{12}$ $\dfrac{4}{24}$ **(1 mark)**

....

2 Insert the symbol **=**, **>** or **<** to make these statements correct.

a. $\dfrac{5}{8}$ ☐ $\dfrac{1}{2}$ **(1 mark)**

b. $\dfrac{17}{20}$ ☐ $\dfrac{35}{40}$ **(1 mark)**

c. $\dfrac{5}{6}$ ☐ $\dfrac{15}{18}$ **(1 mark)**

d. $\dfrac{4}{7}$ ☐ $\dfrac{5}{9}$ **(1 mark)**

3 Circle the largest fraction.

a. $\dfrac{1}{6}$ $\dfrac{1}{2}$ $\dfrac{6}{8}$ $\dfrac{3}{5}$ **(1 mark)**

b. $\dfrac{2}{7}$ $\dfrac{4}{8}$ $\dfrac{3}{9}$ $\dfrac{2}{5}$ **(1 mark)**

c. $\dfrac{1}{4}$ $\dfrac{1}{8}$ $\dfrac{4}{6}$ $\dfrac{2}{3}$ **(1 mark)**

d. $\dfrac{2}{6}$ $\dfrac{4}{8}$ $\dfrac{1}{3}$ $\dfrac{3}{9}$ **(1 mark)**

Adding fractions

1 Calculate:

a. $\dfrac{1}{5} + \dfrac{2}{5} =$ ....   **(1 mark)**

b. $\dfrac{2}{7} + \dfrac{3}{7} + \dfrac{4}{7} =$ ....   **(1 mark)**

c. $\dfrac{1}{8} + \dfrac{3}{4} =$ ....   **(1 mark)**

d. $\dfrac{1}{16} + \dfrac{1}{8} + \dfrac{1}{4} =$ ....   **(1 mark)**

Subtracting fractions

1 Calculate:

a. $\dfrac{4}{8} - \dfrac{1}{8} =$ .... **(1 mark)**

b. $\dfrac{15}{24} - \dfrac{5}{12} =$ .... **(1 mark)**

c. $\dfrac{6}{7} - \dfrac{3}{5} =$ .... **(1 mark)**

d. $\dfrac{97}{100} - \dfrac{8}{10} =$ .... **(1 mark)**

Adding and subtracting mixed numbers

1 Calculate:

a. $1\dfrac{1}{2} + 2\dfrac{1}{2} =$ .... **(1 mark)**

b. $3\dfrac{5}{7} - 1\dfrac{6}{7} =$ .... **(1 mark)**

c. $4\dfrac{2}{6} + 3\dfrac{2}{8} =$ .... **(1 mark)**

d. $3\dfrac{1}{4} - 2\dfrac{1}{5} =$ .... **(1 mark)**

Top tip!

Remember that you can only add and subtract fractions that have the same denominators. So first you will have to convert one or both of them to equivalent fractions with common denominators.

Total $\dfrac{}{22}$

Fractions, Decimals and Percentages

Fractions of an amount

1. Find:

   a. $\frac{1}{2}$ of 540 = ... **(1 mark)**

   b. $\frac{1}{4}$ of 620 = ... **(1 mark)**

   c. $\frac{2}{3}$ of 450 = ... **(1 mark)**

   d. $\frac{1}{4}$ of £8.60 = ... **(1 mark)**

   e. $\frac{2}{3}$ of £3.90 = ... **(1 mark)**

   f. $\frac{2}{7}$ of 5600 ml = ... **(1 mark)**

2. Fill in more squares on this pattern so that $\frac{2}{3}$ are coloured blue. **(1 mark)**

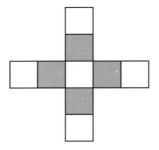

3. Ed buys this chocolate bar. He gives two-thirds to Joe and then eats a quarter of what is left.

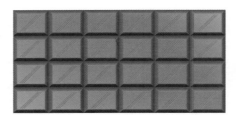

   How many pieces remain? **(1 mark)**

   ....

Multiplying and dividing fractions

1. Calculate:

   a. $\frac{1}{2} \times \frac{1}{4}$ = ... **(1 mark)**   **b.** $\frac{2}{3} \times \frac{4}{8}$ = ... **(1 mark)**

   c. $\frac{1}{2} \times \frac{1}{3}$ = ... **(1 mark)**   **d.** $\frac{4}{6} \times \frac{5}{7}$ = ... **(1 mark)**

   e. $\frac{4}{7} \div 2$ = ... **(1 mark)**   **f.** $\frac{4}{5} \div 2$ = ... **(1 mark)**

Solving problems

1 Rubina bought some cherries. She ate three-quarters of them and put what was left into a bowl. There are seven cherries in the bowl. How many cherries did she buy? **(1 mark)**

> **Top tip!**
> To find fractions of an amount, divide the amount by the denominator and multiply by the numerator.

....

....

2 Jemima has a collection of cuddly toys. She gives $\frac{3}{4}$ of her collection to a charity shop and $\frac{1}{8}$ to her younger sister. She has two cuddly toys left. How many toys were in her collection? **(1 mark)**

....

....

3 360 people enter a fun run. Between three-quarters and four-fifths of the runners complete the run.

Fay says that 282 runners completed the run. Could she be right? Tick Yes or No, then explain how you know. **(2 marks)**

Yes ☐   No ☐   ....

....

4 For school lunch the children can choose pasta, jacket potato or curry. The school cook serves 448 meals. Five-eighths of the children choose pasta and $\frac{3}{16}$ choose jacket potatoes. How many children choose curry? **(2 marks)**

....

....

5 Freddie spent a fifth of his pocket money and has £5.20 left. Omar spent a quarter of his pocket money and has £5.25 left. Which boy receives the most pocket money? Explain how you know. **(2 marks)**

....

....

Total $\frac{}{22}$

Decimal place value

1 Write the value of each red digit.

   a. 0.673 .... **(1 mark)**

   b. 92.085 .... **(1 mark)**

   c. 22.9 .... **(1 mark)**

   d. 0.01 .... **(1 mark)**

2 Calculate:

   a. $0.45 \times 10 =$ .... **(1 mark)**

   b. $0.056 \times 10 =$ .... **(1 mark)**

   c. $0.76 \times 100 =$ .... **(1 mark)**

   d. $0.082 \times 100 =$ .... **(1 mark)**

   e. $0.65 \div 10 =$ .... **(1 mark)**

   f. $0.23 \div 100 =$ .... **(1 mark)**

Comparing decimals

1 Circle all the numbers that are greater than 0.7 **(1 mark)**

   0.66   0.71   0.077   0.59   0.9

2 Circle all the numbers that are less than 0.7 **(1 mark)**

   0.714   0.69   0.07   0.703   0.56

3 Write these numbers in order, starting with the smallest. **(1 mark)**

   9.13   1.91   9.818   8.214   7.28

4 Circle the number that is closest in value to 0.8 **(1 mark)**

   0.82   0.79   0.08   0.88   0.008

Rounding decimals

1 Round these decimals to the nearest tenth.

   a. 5.58 .... **(1 mark)**

   b. 10.59 .... **(1 mark)**

   c. 63.90 .... **(1 mark)**

   d. 17.0144 .... **(1 mark)**

2 Round these numbers to two decimal places.

   a. 1.483 .... **(1 mark)**

   b. 15.3651 .... **(1 mark)**

   c. 24.195 .... **(1 mark)**

   d. 67.341 .... **(1 mark)**

Solving problems

1 Sadie has thought of a three-digit decimal number. She says, "When I round it to the nearest whole number it is three but when I round it to the nearest tenth it is 3.4."

What could Sadie's number be? **(1 mark)**

....

2 When Mr Davis rounded the contents of his shopping trolley to the nearest pound it was £56.
What was the least and the most his shopping could have cost him when he got to the till? **(1 mark)**

....

Total $\frac{}{24}$

Decimal and fraction equivalents

1 Write these fractions as decimals.

a. $\frac{1}{2}$ = ... **(1 mark)**

b. $\frac{1}{4}$ = ... **(1 mark)**

c. $\frac{3}{4}$ = ... **(1 mark)**

d. $\frac{1}{5}$ = ... **(1 mark)**

e. $\frac{14}{100}$ = ... **(1 mark)**

f. $\frac{7}{20}$ = ... **(1 mark)**

g. $\frac{1}{50}$ = ... **(1 mark)**

h. $\frac{6}{8}$ = ... **(1 mark)**

2 **a.** $\frac{3}{8}$ as a decimal fraction is 0.375.

Round it to two decimal places. **(1 mark)**

....

b. $\frac{6}{7}$ as a decimal fraction is 0.85714285714286

Round it to three decimal places. **(1 mark)**

....

Ordering fractions and decimals

1 Write these in order of size, starting with the smallest.

a. $\frac{3}{4}$ $\frac{2}{3}$ $\frac{1}{8}$ 0.67 **(1 mark)**

b. $\frac{1}{2}$ 0.95 $\frac{1}{7}$ 0.210 **(1 mark)**

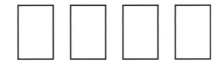

2 Which is greater, 0.6 or $\frac{5}{6}$? .... **(1 mark)**

3 Insert one of the symbols **=**, **<** or **>** to make each statement correct

    a. $\frac{1}{3}$ ☐ 0.3 **(1 mark)**

    b. $\frac{15}{28}$ ☐ 0.5 **(1 mark)**

    c. 0.025 ☐ $\frac{25}{100}$ **(1 mark)**

    d. $\frac{6}{8}$ ☐ 0.75 **(1 mark)**

Decimals, fractions and percentages

1 Convert these percentages to decimal fractions.

    a. 45.5% = ... **(1 mark)**

    b. 5% = ... **(1 mark)**

    c. 75% = ... **(1 mark)**

    d. 1.5% = ... **(1 mark)**

2 Convert these decimal fractions to percentages.

    a. 0.65 = ... **(1 mark)**

    b. 0.01 = ... **(1 mark)**

    c. 0.025 = ... **(1 mark)**

    d. 0.905 = ... **(1 mark)**

3 Circle the odd one out in each set of fractions, decimals and percentages.

    a. $\frac{2}{8}$ $\frac{25}{10}$ $\frac{250}{1000}$ 0.25 **(1 mark)**

    b. 30%   0.333 $\frac{6}{20}$ $\frac{30}{100}$ **(1 mark)**

    c. 0.15 $\frac{30}{200}$ 15% $\frac{15}{50}$ **(1 mark)**

    d. 0.1   1% $\frac{10}{100}$ 10% **(1 mark)**

Total $\frac{}{29}$

Multiplying decimals

1 Calculate:

a.
$$\begin{array}{r} 0.8 \\ \times\ \ \ 5 \\ \hline \\ \hline \end{array}$$
(1 mark)

b.
$$\begin{array}{r} 0.04 \\ \times\ \ \ \ 6 \\ \hline \\ \hline \end{array}$$
(1 mark)

c.
$$\begin{array}{r} 3.45 \\ \times\ \ \ \ 8 \\ \hline \\ \hline \end{array}$$
(1 mark)

d.
$$\begin{array}{r} 5.32 \\ \times\ \ \ \ 4 \\ \hline \\ \hline \end{array}$$
(1 mark)

2 Use these number cards to make both of these equations correct. **(2 marks)**

£ ☐ . 6 0 × 2 = £ 9 . ☐ 0

£ 6 . 3 0 × 0 . ☐ = £ ☐ . 1 5

Dividing decimals

1 **a.** 4)4.64
(1 mark)

b. 3)7.74
(1 mark)

c. 6)56.34
(1 mark)

d. 12)4.8
(1 mark)

2 Use these number cards to make both of these equations correct.

(2 marks)

$$\boxed{5} \quad \boxed{6} \quad \boxed{7} \quad \boxed{8}$$

$\boxed{}\,6\,0 \div 0\,.\,7 = \boxed{}\,0\,0$

$5\,.\,\boxed{} \div \boxed{} = 0\,.\,8$

Solving problems

1 **a.** The 27 children in Year 6 each need a 2.8 m length of rope for Forest School.
How much rope will the leader have to provide?

(1 mark)

....

....

b. Rope is sold in 30 m coils that cost £9.78 each.
How much will their teacher need to spend?

(2 marks)

....

....

2 India buys a pack of 12 multi-coloured gel pens for £6.96. Anna chooses eight individual pens and spends £4.96.
How much more did one of Anna's pens cost?

(2 marks)

....

....

Total $\dfrac{}{17}$

Proportion

1 In a football sticker album, one in every 13 stickers is a club badge. There are 260 stickers in a completed album. How many of them will be club badges? **(1 mark)**

....

....

2 There are 32 chocolates in a packet of Nutz. The proportion of hazelnut chocolates is one in every four. How many hazelnut chocolates would you expect there to be in one packet? **(1 mark)**

....

....

3 After Year 6 completed a traffic survey, they noticed that one in every six vehicles driving past their school was a lorry or a van. In an hour they had counted 43 lorries and vans. How many vehicles had driven past the school altogether in this time? **(1 mark)**

....

....

4 In a 490 g bag of fruit salad, two in every seven pieces of fruit are pineapple chunks. If all the fruit pieces were the same weight, what might you expect to be the weight of pineapple? **(1 mark)**

....

....

5 There are 24 children in class J1. Five out of every eight are girls. There are 27 children in class J2. Four out of every nine are girls.

Myla is in class J1. She says, 'There are more girls in my class than in class, J2'.

Is she right? Tick Yes or No.

Yes ☐   No ☐

Explain how you know.   **(2 marks)**

Proportion compares a part of the whole to the whole whereas ratio compares different parts of the whole to each other.

Top tip!

....

....

Ratio

1 A builder mixes cement with sand and gravel in the weight ratio of one part cement to two parts sand to three parts gravel. He uses 30 kg of sand. How much cement and gravel will he need? **(1 mark)**

....

....

2 A builder is making a patio from coloured and white hexagonal tiles.

Shade some more tiles in so that the ratio of coloured to plain tiles is 3:1. **(1 mark)**

3 Three species of bird visit a bird table: starlings, chaffinches and house sparrows. In an hour Ruth counts the visits by these species to the table and records them in a table.

Species	Number of Visits
Starling	10
Chaffinch	25
House sparrow	5

a. What is the ratio of visits of starlings to chaffinches to house sparrows, reduced to its simplest terms?

☐ : ☐ : ☐   **(1 mark)**

b. On another day Ruth counts 24 visits to the table. If the ratio of visits by the different species remains the same, how many of these would she expect to be made by chaffinches? **(1 mark)**

....

....

4 Kieran is making a smoothie with apple juice, banana purée and yogurt. The ratio by volume of these ingredients is 10 parts apple juice to eight parts banana purée to three parts yogurt. Kieran uses 1200 ml of apple juice.

How much smoothie is Kieran making? **(1 mark)**

....

....

Total ─── 11

Percentages of an amount

1 Calculate:

   a. 1% of 700 = ...   **(1 mark)**

   b. 10% of £34 = ...   **(1 mark)**

   c. 85% of 12 000 = ...   **(1 mark)**

   d. 49% of 500 = ...   **(1 mark)**

   e. 60% of £3.20 = ...   **(1 mark)**

   f. 25% of 1.5 km = ...   **(1 mark)**

2 Shade 40 percent of this pattern.   **(1 mark)**

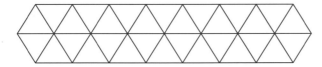

3 What percentage of this totem is shaded?   **(1 mark)**

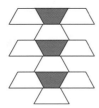

....

4 Tom ate 60 percent of a chocolate bar. This is what he has left.

How many pieces has Tom eaten?   **(1 mark)**

....

Raising and lowering prices

1 Raise these prices by 10 percent.

   a. £4.50 = ... **(1 mark)**

   b. 60p = ... **(1 mark)**

   c. £32 500 = ... **(1 mark)**

   d. £78.90 = ... **(1 mark)**

2 Reduce these prices by 20 percent.

   a. 70p = ... **(1 mark)**

   b. £5.90 = ... **(1 mark)**

   c. £345 900 = ... **(1 mark)**

   d. £88.80 = ... **(1 mark)**

3 Mr Khan is looking for a cheap new TV. At 'Clickvision' the cheapest TV was £457 but has been reduced by 5 percent. At 'Screensavers' the cheapest TV was £470 but is now 10 percent cheaper. Where will Mr Khan find the cheapest TV?

Circle the shop with the cheapest TV.

Clickvision / Screensavers

Explain how you know. **(2 marks)**

....

....

4 Jen's flat is for sale at £160 000.
After a week the estate agents reduce the price by 10 percent.

   a. What is the new reduced price? **(1 mark)**

   ....

   b. After the flat is sold, Jen has to pay the estate agents 2 percent of the sale price. How much is this? **(1 mark)**

   ....

Total $\frac{}{21}$

Similar shapes

❶ Look at triangle ABC. On the grid draw a similar triangle that is:

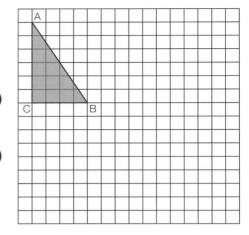

a. two times larger than triangle ABC **(1 mark)**

b. half the size of triangle ABC **(1 mark)**

❷ Look at this rectangle.

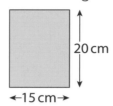

20 cm

←15 cm→

The length and width of this rectangle are five times larger than a similar rectangle. What is the area of the smaller rectangle? **(1 mark)**

....

Scale factor

❶ Mrs Chant is redesigning her garden. She has made a scale drawing. The drawing has a scale of 1:50.

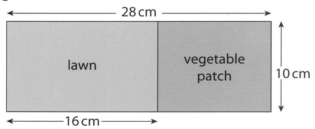

a. How long is Mrs Chant's actual garden? **(1 mark)**

....

b. What area of her garden has Mrs Chant planned to use as a vegetable patch? **(1 mark)**

....

❷ Harrison has a 1:300 scale model of a battleship. The battleship that Harrison's model is based upon was 252 m long.

a. How long is Harrison's model? **(1 mark)**

....

NUMBERS

Place value
pages 4–5

Place value
1 a. 60 (1 mark)
   b. 700 (1 mark)
   c. 9 (1 mark)
   d. 4000 (1 mark)
   e. 6000 (1 mark)
   f. 10000 (1 mark)
   g. 30000 (1 mark)
   h. 300000 (1 mark)
2 a. 954321 (1 mark)
   b. 123459 (1 mark)

Ordering numbers
1 a. 212 221 2021 2120 12120
      21210 (1 mark)
   b. 667 766 6607 6670 66707
      67706 (1 mark)
2 a. 33311 31313 3311 3113 331
      313 (1 mark)
   b. 14994 14494 1944 1499 949
      449 (1 mark)

Greater than and less than
1 a. 4600 > 4060 (1 mark)
   b. 10033 < 10303 (1 mark)
   c. 12269 < 12469 (1 mark)
   d. 423486 < 432008 (1 mark)
2 a. 120 + 60 = 200 − 20 (1 mark)
   b. 350 + 60 > 700 − 360 (1 mark)
   c. 1200 − 300 > 10 × 80 (1 mark)
   d. 0.9 + 0.2 < 4.8 ÷ 4 (1 mark)

Numbers in words
1 a. twelve thousand four hundred and five (1 mark)
   b. eight million four hundred and two thousand
      seven hundred and ninety eight (1 mark)
   c. three hundred and twelve thousand
      and nine (1 mark)
2 a. 28602 (1 mark)
   b. 602736 (1 mark)
   c. 1000511 (1 mark)

Rounding and negative numbers
pages 6–7

Rounding numbers
1 a. 70 (1 mark)
   b. 80 (1 mark)
   c. 100 (1 mark)
   d. 19900 (1 mark)
2 a. 700 (1 mark)
   b. 400 (1 mark)
   c. 2000 (1 mark)

   d. 56900 (1 mark)
3 a. 1000 (1 mark)
   b. 32000 (1 mark)
   c. 130000 (1 mark)
   d. 1340000 (1 mark)
4 a. 74890 (1 mark)
   b. 74900 (1 mark)
   c. 75000 (1 mark)

Rounding money
1 a. £34.00 (1 mark)
   b. £1.00 (1 mark)
   c. £1640.00 (1 mark)
   d. £9.00 (1 mark)
2 £35 + £27 + £45 = £107
      **(2 marks: award 2 marks for correct answer and
      rounding; only award 1 mark for evidence of
      correct method with one arithmetical error)**

Negative numbers
1 a. 9 (1 mark)
   b. −31 (1 mark)
   c. 13 (1 mark)
   d. −4 (1 mark)
2 a. 32°C (1 mark)
   b. −£4 (1 mark)

CALCULATIONS

Order of operations
pages 8–9

BIDMAS
1 a. 3 (1 mark)
   b. 121 (1 mark)
   c. 5 (1 mark)
   d. 4400 (1 mark)
2 A – the total is 29.5
   B – the total is 57 so B is greater
      **(2 marks: award 2 marks for B with correct
      explanation; only award 1 mark if B is selected but
      no explanation)**

Missing symbol
1 a. < (1 mark)
   b. = (1 mark)
   c. > (1 mark)
   d. = (1 mark)

Missing numbers
1 a. 40 (1 mark)
   b. 6 (1 mark)
   c. 20 (1 mark)
2 a. Various answers are possible,
      e.g. 4 and 100. (1 mark)
   b. Accept any two numbers with a
      product of 20. (1 mark)

Missing brackets

1 **a.** $(52 - 3) \div 7 = 42 \div 6$ **(1 mark)**
   b. $225 \div 5 = (3 + 2) \times 9$ **(1 mark)**
   c. $(2 + 3) \times 4 + 5 \times 6 = 50$ **(1 mark)**
   d. $7 + 6 \times (5 + 4) = \dfrac{122}{2}$ **(1 mark)**

Factors and multiples
pages 10–11

Multiples

1 108 126 **(1 mark)**

2 72 702 8022 **(1 mark)**

3 5005 **(1 mark)**
4 96 **(1 mark)**
5 120 **(1 mark)**
6 12 and 48 OR 24 and 36 **(1 mark)**
7 4 and 2 (accept 1) **(1 mark)**

8 Accept 'No' together with an example that shows this is not always correct, for example 3 × 3 equals 9 and 9 is not a multiple of 6. **(1 mark)**

Factors

1 **a.**

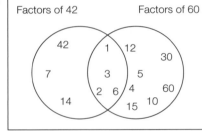

Factors of 42   Factors of 60

42   1 12   30
7   3   5
      2 6 4   60
14   15 10

(2 marks: 2 marks for Venn diagram completed as illustrated with 14 numbers placed correctly; 1 mark for 12 numbers placed correctly)
   b. 1, 2, 3 and 6 **(1 mark)**
   c. 6 **(1 mark)**
2. Accept any square number, for example 4, 9, 36. **(1 mark)**
3. 24
4. 19 and 23 **(1 mark)**
5. 1, 2, 13 and 26 **(1 mark)**
6. **a.** 5 and 7 **(1 mark)**
    b. 3 and 13 **(1 mark)**

Addition
pages 12–13

Addition with whole numbers

1 **a.** 104 **(1 mark)**
   b. 171 **(1 mark)**
   c. 750 **(1 mark)**
   d. 10 044 **(1 mark)**

2 **a.** 2899 **(1 mark)**
   b. 8474 **(1 mark)**
   c. 11 865 **(1 mark)**
   d. 68 746 **(1 mark)**

Addition with decimals

1 **a.** 4 **(1 mark)**
   b. 53 **(1 mark)**
   c. 4.3 **(1 mark)**
   d. £12 **(1 mark)**
2 **a.** £306.66 **(1 mark)**
   b. 46.65 m **(1 mark)**
   c. 1.83 litres **(1 mark)**
   d. 192.561 **(1 mark)**

Solving problems

1 **a.** 22 **(1 mark)**
   b. 13 **(1 mark)**
2 580 miles **(1 mark)**
3 4.8 metres **(1 mark)**
4 £32 and £17 **(1 mark)**
5 £14.75 **(1 mark)**

Subtraction
pages 14–15

Small differences

1 **a.** 5 **(1 mark)**
   b. 13 cm **(1 mark)**
   c. 16 **(1 mark)**
   d. £0.06 **(1 mark)**

Subtraction with whole numbers

1 **a.** 2210 **(1 mark)**
   b. 5029 **(1 mark)**
   c. 6554 **(1 mark)**
   d. 4605 **(1 mark)**

Subtraction with decimals

1 **a.** 2 **(1 mark)**
   b. 9.4 **(1 mark)**
   c. £90.99 **(1 mark)**
   d. 0.05 cm **(1 mark)**
2 **a.** 2.219 **(1 mark)**
   b. £21.95 **(1 mark)**
   c. 4.203 **(1 mark)**
   d. 112.644 **(1 mark)**

Solving problems

1 355.64 miles **(1 mark)**
2 £3.10 **(1 mark)**
3 12.47 seconds **(1 mark)**
4 900 ml **(1 mark)**
5 40p **(1 mark)**
6 130 cm **(1 mark)**

Multiplication

pages 16–17

Grid method

1. a. 19 140   **(1 mark)**
   b. 45 288   **(1 mark)**
   c. 39 264   **(1 mark)**
   d. 426 964   **(1 mark)**

Short multiplication

1. a. 3045   **(1 mark)**
   b. 1148   **(1 mark)**
   c. 37 050   **(1 mark)**
   d. 74 754   **(1 mark)**

Long multiplication

1. a. 9632   **(1 mark)**
   b. 30 084   **(1 mark)**
   c. 75 858   **(1 mark)**
   d. 35 955   **(1 mark)**

Solving problems

1. £240   **(1 mark)**
2. a. 700   **(1 mark)**
   b. £175   **(1 mark)**
3. £535.20   **(1 mark)**
4. £297   **(1 mark)**

5.   **(1 mark)**

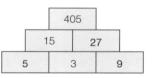

Division

pages 18–19

Short division

1. a. 231   **(1 mark)**
   b. 108   **(1 mark)**
   c. 715   **(1 mark)**
   d. 908   **(1 mark)**

Long division

1. a. 37   **(1 mark)**
   b. 22   **(1 mark)**
   c. 194   **(1 mark)**
   d. 65   **(1 mark)**

Remainders

1. a. $132\frac{3}{4}$ **(1 mark)**
   b. $317\frac{5}{6}$ **(1 mark)**
2. a. 14.4   **(1 mark)**
   b. 555.25   **(1 mark)**

Problem solving

1. 14   **(1 mark)**

2. 9   **(1 mark)**
3. 38   **(1 mark)**
4. a. 14   **(1 mark)**
   b. £3920   **(1 mark)**

Problem solving

pages 20–21

Multi-step problems

1. £35.25   **(2 marks)**
2. £7.07   **(2 marks)**
3. 50p   **(2 marks)**
4. a. £5.50   **(2 marks)**
   b. £3.50   **(2 marks)**
5. 65   **(2 marks)**

   For questions 1–5 above, award 1 mark for evidence of appropriate working with one arithmetical error allowed, and 1 mark for correct answer.

6. a. £575   **(1 mark)**
   b. 15   **(1 mark)**

Arithmetic

pages 22–23

Addition, subtraction, multiplication and division

1. 1023   **(1 mark)**
2. 143.355   **(1 mark)**
3. 255   **(1 mark)**
4. 112   **(1 mark)**
5. 398   **(1 mark)**
6. 2.07   **(1 mark)**

Times tables

pages 24–25

Multiplication grids

1.

×	8	3	9	5	10	12
4	32	12	36	20	40	48
11	88	33	99	55	110	132
6	48	18	54	30	60	72
7	56	21	63	35	70	84
2	16	6	18	10	20	24

(2 marks: award the full 2 marks for 30 correct answers; 1 mark for 22–29 correct answers)

2. a.

×	7	8	9
2	14	16	18
3	21	24	27
4	28	32	36

      (1 mark)

b.

×	5	7	9
2	10	**14**	18
4	**20**	**28**	36
6	30	42	**54**

(1 mark)

c.

×	11	**12**	**10**
9	99	108	**90**
8	88	96	80
7	77	84	**70**

(1 mark)

Time yourself

1 21
2 11
3 12
4 44
5 30
6 16
7 6
8 90
9 32
10 22
11 99
12 88
13 80
14 54
15 88
16 55
17 16
18 28
19 64
20 66
21 120
22 6
23 6
24 70
25 72
26 60
27 40
28 54
29 12
30 36
31 33
32 77
33 120
34 24
35 36
36 56
37 12
38 36
39 48
40 8

41 108
42 132
43 20
44 7
45 45
46 72
47 45
48 42
49 20
50 84
51 96
52 56
53 22
54 40
55 90
56 54
57 99
58 12
59 10
60 24

(4 marks: award the full 4 marks for all correct; −1 mark for each mistake)

FRACTIONS, DECIMALS AND PERCENTAGES

Fractions
pages 26–27

Equivalent fractions

1 a. $\frac{2}{6}$ (1 mark)

   b. $\frac{1}{2}$ (1 mark)

   c. $\frac{8}{10}$ (1 mark)

   d. $\frac{1}{4}$ (1 mark)

   e. $\frac{2}{3}$ (1 mark)

   f. $\frac{3}{5}$ (1 mark)

2 a. $\frac{1}{4} = \frac{3}{12} = \frac{6}{24} = \frac{12}{48}$ (1 mark)

   b. $\frac{1}{3} = \frac{2}{6} = \frac{4}{12} = \frac{8}{24}$ (1 mark)

3 a. $\frac{20}{100}$ (1 mark)

   b. $\frac{30}{42}$ (1 mark)

Reducing fractions

1 a. $\dfrac{5}{8}$ (1 mark)

 b. $\dfrac{3}{4}$ (1 mark)

 c. $\dfrac{3}{4}$ (1 mark)

 d. $\dfrac{3}{5}$ (1 mark)

Mixed numbers and improper fractions

1 a. $5\dfrac{2}{5}$ (1 mark)

 b. $7\dfrac{1}{6}$ (1 mark)

 c. $6\dfrac{2}{9}$ (1 mark)

 d. $8\dfrac{7}{8}$ (1 mark)

2 a. $\dfrac{19}{4}$ (1 mark)

 b. $\dfrac{62}{7}$ (1 mark)

 c. $\dfrac{101}{10}$ (1 mark)

 d. $\dfrac{23}{3}$ (1 mark)

3 a. = (1 mark)
 b. > (1 mark)
 c. > (1 mark)
 d. = (1 mark)

Operations with fractions
pages 28–29

Ordering fractions

1 a. $\dfrac{1}{3}$ $\dfrac{1}{2}$ $\dfrac{7}{12}$ $\dfrac{5}{6}$ (1 mark)

 b. $\dfrac{4}{24}$ $\dfrac{4}{8}$ $\dfrac{3}{4}$ $\dfrac{10}{12}$ (1 mark)

2 a. > (1 mark)
 b. < (1 mark)
 c. = (1 mark)
 d. > (1 mark)

3 a. $\boxed{\dfrac{6}{8}}$ (1 mark)

 b. $\boxed{\dfrac{4}{8}}$ (1 mark)

 c. $\boxed{\dfrac{4}{6}}$ or $\boxed{\dfrac{2}{3}}$ (1 mark)

 d. $\boxed{\dfrac{4}{8}}$ (1 mark)

Adding fractions

1 a. $\dfrac{3}{5}$ (1 mark)

 b. $1\dfrac{2}{7}$, accept $\dfrac{9}{7}$ (1 mark)

 c. $\dfrac{7}{8}$ (1 mark)

 d. $\dfrac{7}{16}$ (1 mark)

Subtracting fractions

1 a. $\dfrac{3}{8}$ (1 mark)

 b. $\dfrac{5}{24}$ (1 mark)

 c. $\dfrac{9}{35}$ (1 mark)

 d. $\dfrac{17}{100}$ (1 mark)

Adding and subtracting mixed numbers

1 a. 4 (1 mark)

 b. $1\dfrac{6}{7}$ (1 mark)

 c. $7\dfrac{7}{12}$ or $7\dfrac{14}{24}$ (1 mark)

 d. $1\dfrac{1}{20}$ (1 mark)

Fractions of an amount
pages 30–31

Fractions of an amount

1 a. 270 (1 mark)
 b. 155 (1 mark)
 c. 300 (1 mark)
 d. £2.15 (1 mark)
 e. £2.60 (1 mark)
 f. 1600 ml (1 mark)
2 Any two extra squares shaded. (1 mark)
3 Six pieces remain. (1 mark)

Multiplying and dividing fractions

1 a. $\dfrac{1}{8}$ (1 mark)

 b. $\dfrac{8}{24}$ (1 mark)

 c. $\dfrac{1}{6}$ (1 mark)

 d. $\dfrac{20}{42}$ (1 mark)

 e. $\dfrac{4}{14}$ (1 mark)

 f. $\dfrac{4}{10}$ (1 mark)

Solving problems

1 28 (1 mark)
2 16 (1 mark)
3 Yes. You can work out that between 270 and 288 runners completed the course. **(2 marks: award 2 marks for Yes with an explanation that recognises that between 270 and 288 runners completed the course, but only 1 mark for Yes without an explanation)**
4 84 **(2 marks: 1 mark for evidence of appropriate working with one arithmetical error allowed, 1 mark for correct answer)**
5 Omar. Freddie gets £6.50 and Omar £7.00 **(2 marks: award 2 marks for Omar with an explanation that recognises that Freddie gets £6.50 and Omar gets £7.00; only award 1 mark for Omar with no explanation)**

Decimals
pages 32–33

Decimal place value

1 a. seven-hundredths (1 mark)
   b. five-thousandths (1 mark)
   c. nine-tenths (1 mark)
   d. one-hundredth (1 mark)
2 a. 4.5 (1 mark)
   b. 0.56 (1 mark)
   c. 76 (1 mark)
   d. 8.2 (1 mark)
   e. 0.065 (1 mark)
   f. 0.0023 (1 mark)

Comparing decimals

1 (0.71) (0.9) (1 mark)
2 (0.69) (0.07) (0.56) (1 mark)
3 1.91 7.28 8.214 9.13 9.818 (1 mark)
4 (0.79) (1 mark)

Rounding decimals

1 a. 5.6 (1 mark)
   b. 10.6 (1 mark)
   c. 63.9 (1 mark)
   d. 17.0 (1 mark)
2 a. 1.48 (1 mark)
   b. 15.37 (1 mark)
   c. 24.20 (1 mark)
   d. 67.34 (1 mark)

Solving problems

1 Accept any three-digit decimal in the range 3.35 to 3.44. (1 mark)
2 £55.50 and £56.49 **(1 mark for both)**

Decimal and fraction equivalents
pages 34–35

Decimal and fraction equivalents

1 a. 0.5 (1 mark)
   b. 0.25 (1 mark)
   c. 0.75 (1 mark)
   d. 0.2 (1 mark)
   e. 0.14 (1 mark)
   f. 0.35 (1 mark)
   g. 0.02 (1 mark)
   h. 0.75 (1 mark)
2 a. 0.38 (1 mark)
   b. 0.857 (1 mark)

Ordering fractions and decimals

1 a. $\frac{1}{8}$ $\frac{2}{3}$ 0.67 $\frac{3}{4}$ (1 mark)
   b. $\frac{1}{7}$ 0.210 $\frac{1}{2}$ 0.95 (1 mark)
2 $\frac{5}{6}$ **(1 mark)**
3 a. > (1 mark)
   b. > (1 mark)
   c. < (1 mark)
   d. = (1 mark)

Decimals, fractions and percentages

1 a. 0.455 (1 mark)
   b. 0.05 (1 mark)
   c. 0.75 (1 mark)
   d. 0.015 (1 mark)
2 a. 65% (1 mark)
   b. 1% (1 mark)
   c. 2.5% (1 mark)
   d. 90.5% (1 mark)
3 a. $\frac{25}{10}$ (1 mark)
   b. 0.333 (1 mark)
   c. $\frac{15}{50}$ (1 mark)
   d. 1% (1 mark)

Multiplying and dividing decimals
pages 36–37

Multiplying decimals

1 a. 4 (1 mark)
   b. 0.24 (1 mark)
   c. 27.6 (1 mark)
   d. 21.28 (1 mark)
2 £4.60 × 2 = £9.20
   £6.30 × 0.5 = £3.15
   (2 marks: award 2 marks for all four cards correct, but only 1 mark for two correct cards)

Dividing decimals

1 a.
$$4 \overline{)\begin{array}{c} 1.16 \\ 4.64 \end{array}}$$
(1 mark)

b.
$$3 \overline{)\begin{array}{c} 2.58 \\ 7.74 \end{array}}$$
(1 mark)

c.
$$6 \overline{)\begin{array}{c} 9.39 \\ 56.34 \end{array}}$$
(1 mark)

d.
$$12 \overline{)\begin{array}{c} 0.4 \\ 4.8 \end{array}}$$
(1 mark)

2 **5**60 ÷ 0.7 = **8**00
5.**6** ÷ **7** = 0.8
(2 marks: award 2 marks for all four cards correct but only 1 mark for two correct cards)

Solving problems

1 a. 75.6 m **(1 mark)**

b. £29.34 **(2 marks: 1 mark for the correct answer, 1 mark for evidence of appropriate working with one arithmetical error allowed)**

2 4p **(1 mark for the correct answer, 1 mark for evidence of appropriate working with one arithmetical error allowed)**

RATIO AND PROPORTION

Ratio and proportion
pages 38–39

Proportion

1 20 **(1 mark)**
2 8 **(1 mark)**
3 258 **(1 mark)**
4 140 g **(1 mark)**

5 Yes ☑ with explanation. **(2 marks: award 2 marks for an explanation that recognises that there would be 15 girls in class J1 but only 12 in class J2; only award 1 mark if Yes is ticked but only one of the two numbers of girls is given)**

Ratio

1 15 kg cement and 45 kg gravel. **(1 mark)**
2 Any nine additional tiles shaded in. **(1 mark)**
3 a. 2 : 5 : 1 **(1 mark)**
b. 15 chaffinches **(1 mark)**
4 2520 ml **(1 mark)**

Percentages
pages 40–41

Percentages of an amount

1 a. 7 **(1 mark)**
b. £3.40 **(1 mark)**
c. 10 200 **(1 mark)**
d. 245 **(1 mark)**

e. £1.92 **(1 mark)**
f. 375 m or 0.375 km **(1 mark)**

2 Accept any 12 triangles shaded. **(1 mark)**
3 25% **(1 mark)**
4 18 pieces **(1 mark)**

Raising and lowering prices

1 a. £4.95 **(1 mark)**
b. 66p **(1 mark)**
c. £35 750 **(1 mark)**
d. £86.79 **(1 mark)**
2 a. 56p **(1 mark)**
b. £4.72 **(1 mark)**
c. £276 720 **(1 mark)**
d. £71.04 **(1 mark)**

3 Screensavers with explanation. **(2 marks: award 2 marks for an explanation that recognises that the TV will cost £434.15 at Clickvision and £423 at Screensavers; only award 1 mark if Screensavers is circled but only one of the reduced prices is given correctly.)**

4 a. £144 000 **(1 mark)**
b. £2880 **(1 mark)**

Scale
pages 42–43

Similar shapes

1 a. Two times larger than triangle ABC **(1 mark)**
b. Half the size of triangle ABC **(1 mark)**

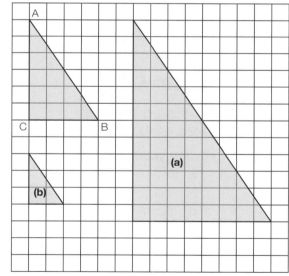

2 12 cm² **(1 mark)**

Scale factor

1 a. 14 m **(1 mark)**
b. 30 m² **(1 mark)**
2 a. 84 cm **(1 mark)**
b. 135 m **(1 mark)**

Distances

1 a.

	Rhos-neigr	Llan-badrig	Moelfre	Llangefni
Rhosneigr		43 km	30 km	17 km
Llanbadrig	43 km		39 km	26 km
Moelfre	30 km	39 km		13 km
Llangefni	17 km	26 km	13 km	

(2 marks: award 2 marks for all 10 missing distances completed correctly; only award 1 mark for 8–9 distances completed correctly)

   b. 32 cm   **(1 mark)**

Solving problems
pages 44–45

Solving problems

1 a. Award 2 marks for an answer that recognises that John Street's library has 255 non-fiction books and Ford Lane's library has 244.   **(2 marks)**

   b. Award 1 mark for the correct answer of 1 in 2 or a half or 50%.   **(1 mark)**

2 22   **(1 mark)**
3 77 900   **(1 mark)**
4 £318.75   **(1 mark)**
5 a. 50%   **(1 mark)**
   b. 13.2 m^2 **(1 mark)**
6 1875 ml   **(1 mark)**
7 One   **(1 mark)**
8 a. 26 km   **(1 mark)**
   b. 104 cm   **(1 mark)**

ALGEBRA

Missing numbers
pages 46–47

Missing numbers

1 a. 44   **(1 mark)**
   b. 120   **(1 mark)**
   c. 66 cm   **(1 mark)**
   d. £10   **(1 mark)**
   e. 9   **(1 mark)**
   f. 98   **(1 mark)**
   g. 5   **(1 mark)**
   h. 34   **(1 mark)**
2 a. 1 and 3   **(1 mark)**
   b. 8 and 4   **(1 mark)**
3 8   **(1 mark)**
4 ■ = 8   **(1 mark)**

Missing angles

1 36°   **(1 mark)**
2 77°   **(1 mark)**

Missing lengths

1 4.5 cm   **(1 mark)**
2 8 cm   **(1 mark)**
3 6 cm   **(1 mark)**

Formulae and equations
pages 48–49

Equations and expressions

1 a. $x = 4$ **(1 mark)**
   b. $x = 5$ **(1 mark)**
   c. $x = 15$ **(1 mark)**
   d. $x = 63$ **(1 mark)**
2 a. 4   **(1 mark)**
   b. 120   **(1 mark)**
   c. 48   **(1 mark)**
   d. 66   **(1 mark)**
3 a. $y = 10$ **(1 mark)**
   b. $x = 4$ **(1 mark)**
   c. $y = 16$ **(1 mark)**
4 $s = 6$, $t = 3$ and $u = 7$ **(2 marks: award 2 marks for all correct answers; only 1 mark for any two letters correct.)**

Formulae

1 $V = LWH$ or $V = L \times W \times H$ (LWH can appear in any order)   **(1 mark)**
2 a. 36 gallons   **(1 mark)**
   b. 8   **(1 mark)**
3

Shape	Number of edges (E)	Number of faces (F)	Number of vertices (V)
Octahedron	12	8	**6**
Dodecahedron	**30**	12	20
Icosahedron	30	**20**	12

(2 marks: 2 marks for all correct answers; 1 mark for two correct answers)

Number patterns
pages 50–51

Number sequences

1 a. 56, 64, 72   **(1 mark)**
   b. −6, −3 , 0   **(1 mark)**
   c. 15, 7.5, 3.75   **(1 mark)**
   d. 937.5, 4687.5, 23437.5   **(1 mark)**
   e. 20, 11, 2   **(1 mark)**
   f. 0, −4, −8   **(1 mark)**

Reasoning about number sequences

1 No, because the other numbers are all multiples of five.   **(1 mark)**
2 11.5   17   22.5   **(1 mark)**

Pattern problems

1 **a.** $p = 3n + 2$ ✓ (1 mark)
 b. 77 m
2 **a.** 26 sides. (1 mark)
 b. $s = 4n + 2$ (1 mark)

MEASUREMENT

Units of measurement
pages 52–53

Length

1 **a.** 1 m 52 cm (1 mark)
 b. 5600 m (1 mark)
 c. 160 mm (1 mark)
 d. 75 cm (1 mark)
 e. 9.8 cm (1 mark)
2 **a.** 600 m (1 mark)
 b. 0.6 km (1 mark)

Mass and Weight

1 **a.** 8 kg (1 mark)
 b. 550 g (1 mark)
 c. 950 g (1 mark)
2 175 g (1 mark)

Capacity

1 **a.** 700 ml (1 mark)
 b. 1.33 litres (1 mark)
 c. 800 ml (1 mark)
2 550 ml (1 mark)

Reading scales

1 **a.** 130 ml (1 mark)
 b. 425 g (1 mark)

Time
pages 54–55

Units of measurement

1 **a.** 140 minutes (1 mark)
 b. 1 minute 25 seconds (1 mark)
 c. 2 hours 30 minutes (1 mark)
 d. 210 seconds (1 mark)

Analogue and digital clocks

1

twenty past seven	twenty to nine	ten past five	ten to four

3.50	5.10	8.40	7.20

 (4 marks: 1 mark for each correct answer)
2 **a.** 6.25 (1 mark)
 b. 8.45 (1 mark)
 c. 11.15 (1 mark)
 d. 4.05 (1 mark)

The 24 hour clock

1 **a.** 02.10 (1 mark)
 b. 16.55 (1 mark)
 c. 18.15 (1 mark)
 d. 06.35 (1 mark)

Time problems

1 46 mins (1 mark)
2 18.10 (1 mark)
3 **a.** (Train 1) 09.15 (1 mark)
 b. (Train 2) 10.20 (1 mark)
 c. 1 hour 16 minutes (1 mark)

Imperial measures
pages 56–57

Length

1 **a.** 12.5 cm (1 mark)
 b. 25 cm (1 mark)
 c. 30 cm (1 mark)
 d. 97.5 cm (1 mark)
2 150 cm (1 mark)
3 24 inches (1 mark)

Weight

1 **a.** 280 g (1 mark)
 b. 900 g (1 mark)
 c. 6300 g (1 mark)
2 3.6 kg (1 mark)
3 11 lb (1 mark)
4 Accept 335–345 g (1 mark)

Conversion graphs

1 **a.** **i.** 56 km (1 mark)
  ii. 35 miles (1 mark)
 b. 44 miles (1 mark)
 c. 27.5 miles (1 mark)

Area and perimeter
pages 58–59

Area of shapes

1 612 cm^2 (1 mark)
2 476 cm^2 (1 mark)
3 112 cm^2 (1 mark)

Compound shapes

1 **a.** 52 m (1 mark)
 b. 123 m^2 (1 mark)

Perimeter

1 48 cm (1 mark)
2 48 cm (1 mark)
3 9 cm (1 mark)
4 8 cm (1 mark)

Volume
pages 60–61

Calculating volume

1 1440 cm^3
 (2 marks: 1 mark for evidence of the correct method with one arithmetical error, 1 mark for correct answer)

2 $42\,m^3$ **(1 mark)**

3 $1728\,cm^3$ **(1 mark)**

Solving problems

1 a. 4 cm   **(1 mark)**

  b. A variety of answers that when multiplied together make $36\,cm^3$ are possible, for example $2\,cm \times 2\,cm \times 9\,cm$ **(1 mark)**

2 a. $25.6\,m^3$ **(1 mark)**

  b. 7   **(1 mark)**

3 A variety of answers are possible, but one option is: $20\,m \times 5\,m \times 8\,m$ **(1 mark)**

4 9 cm   **(1 mark)**

5 $96\,cm^3$ **(1 mark)**

Measurement
pages 62–63

Area

1 $12\,cm^2$ **(1 mark)**

2 $10\,cm^2$ **(1 mark)**

Measuring angles

1 50°   **(1 mark)**

2 130°   **(1 mark)**

Drawing shapes

1 4.3 cm (accept 4.2 cm–4.4 cm) for the missing side and 50 degrees (accept 49–51°) and 75 degrees (accept 74–76°) for the missing angles.
  (2 marks: award the 2 marks for all three values correct; only 1 mark for any two values correct)

2 5.5 cm (accept 5.4–5.6 cm) for the side and 87 degrees (accept 86–88°) and 63 degrees (accept 62–64°) for the two missing angles.
  (2 marks: award the 2 marks for all three values correct; only 1 mark for any two values correct)

GEOMETRY

2D and 3D shapes
pages 64–65

2D shapes

1 A parallelogram   **(1 mark)**

2 A rectangle   **(1 mark)**

3 A kite   **(1 mark)**

Triangles

1

scalene	isosceles	equilateral	right-angled
one right-angle of 90°	two equal sides and two equal angles	no equal sides or angles	all sides and angles are equal

(2 marks: award the 2 marks for all triangles matched correctly; only 1 mark for 3 triangles matched correctly)

3D shapes

1 a. A triangular prism   **(1 mark)**

  b. A square-based pyramid   **(1 mark)**

2 a. A hexagonal prism   **(1 mark)**

  b. Eight faces, 18 edges and 12 vertices   **(1 mark)**

3 Nine   **(1 mark)**

Circles and angles
pages 66–67

Circles and turns

1 a. 24 cm   **(1 mark)**

  b. 75.36 cm   **(1 mark)**

2 a. 22 cm   **(1 mark)**

  b. 138.16 cm   **(1 mark)**

3 a. 90°   **(1 mark)**

  b. 270°   **(1 mark)**

Angles in triangles

1 a. 35°   **(1 mark)**

  b. i. angle a 70°   **(1 mark)**

    ii. angle b 55°   **(1 mark)**

Calculating angles

1 55°   **(1 mark)**

2 137°   **(1 mark)**

3 170°   **(1 mark)**

4 $a = 39°$ **(1 mark)**

   $b = 141°$ **(1 mark)**

Position and direction
pages 68–69

Coordinates

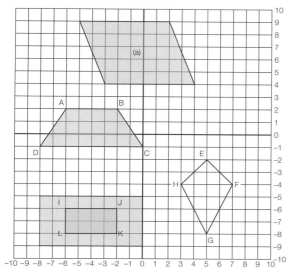

1 a. Parallelogram drawn as illustrated
       on grid.   **(1 mark)**
   b. A(–6, 2) B(–2, 2) C(0, –1) D(–8, –1)

                                                    (1 mark)
   c. *(3, –4)*   **(1 mark)**
   d. A suitable rectangle as illustrated on grid.
       e.g. (–8, –5), (0, –5), (0, –9), (–8, –9)   **(1 mark)**
2 (12, 31)   **(1 mark)**

Reflections and translations

1

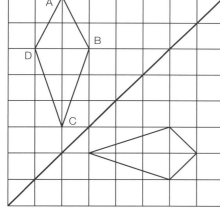

                                                    (1 mark)

2

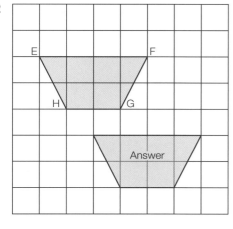

                                                    (1 mark)

STATISTICS

Pie charts
pages 70–71

Understanding pie charts

1 a. 45°   **(1 mark)**
   b. 40   **(1 mark)**
   c. 25%   **(1 mark)**
2 38 more Ash trees
   **(2 marks: 1 mark for evidence of appropriate
   method with one arithmetical error allowed; 1 mark
   for correct answer)**

Drawing pie charts

1

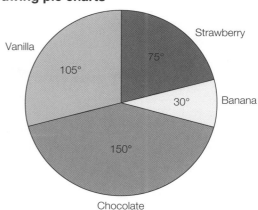

**(3 marks: award the 3 marks for pie chart drawn
and labelled as indicated with angles drawn to
within 2° of the values shown for each sector)**

Line graphs and averages
pages 72–73

Line graphs

1 a. 15°C   **(1 mark)**
   b. 6°C   **(1 mark)**
2 a. Accept answers in the range 86 to 88 Lira
       inclusive.   **(1 mark)**
   b. Accept answers in the range £5.70 to
       £6.00 inclusive.   **(1 mark)**
   c. Accept answers in the range £15.80 to
       £16.20 inclusive.   **(1 mark)**
   d. Accept answers in the range 30–33 Lira
       inclusive.   **(1 mark)**

Averages

1 a. 5   **(1 mark)**
   b. 252   **(1 mark)**
   c. £21.10   **(1 mark)**
   d. 1.5   **(1 mark)**
2 a. $4\frac{1}{2}$ **(1 mark)**
   b. 4   **(1 mark)**
3 5   **(1 mark)**

MIXED PRACTICE QUESTIONS

pages 74–79

1 a. 23°C **(1 mark)**
   b. 29°C **(1 mark)**
2 (0.59) **(1 mark)**
3 1.7   1.78   7.119   7.17   7.2 **(1 mark)**
4 $\dfrac{10}{16}$ **(1 mark)**

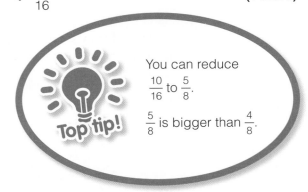

You can reduce $\dfrac{10}{16}$ to $\dfrac{5}{8}$.

$\dfrac{5}{8}$ is bigger than $\dfrac{4}{8}$.

5 $\dfrac{3}{4}$ ✓ $\dfrac{9}{12}$ ✓ **(1 mark)**

6 960 **(1 mark)**
7 90 **(1 mark)**
8 a. 420   480   540 **(1 mark)**
   b. (Yes) **(1 mark)**
   Accept answer such as:
   Used knowledge of six times table.
   Counted in sixes then multiplied by 10.
   Added in multiples of 60. **(1 mark)**

9 9   14   19 **(1 mark)**
10 40 359 **(1 mark)**
11 £2.46 **(1 mark)**
12 a. 255 **(1 mark)**
   b. 585 **(1 mark)**
13 364 **(1 mark)**
14 24 888 **(1 mark)**
15 5184 **(1 mark)**
16 29 r18 **(1 mark)**
17 ($x = 6z$) **(1 mark)**
18 70p **(1 mark)**
19 1295 miles **(1 mark)**
20 70 cm **(1 mark)**
21 Check accuracy of drawing, the height
   should be 4 cm and the base should
   be 6 cm **(1 mark)**
22 a. 10 **(1 mark)**
   b. 25% **(1 mark)**
23 1200 cm³ **(1 mark)**
24 82 m **(1 mark)**

b. Harrison has another 1:300 scale model of a ship that is 45 cm long. How many metres long would the ship that it was modelled on be? **(1 mark)**

....

Distances

❶ These distances come from a 1:50 000 scale map. Two centimetres on the map equals one kilometre on the ground.

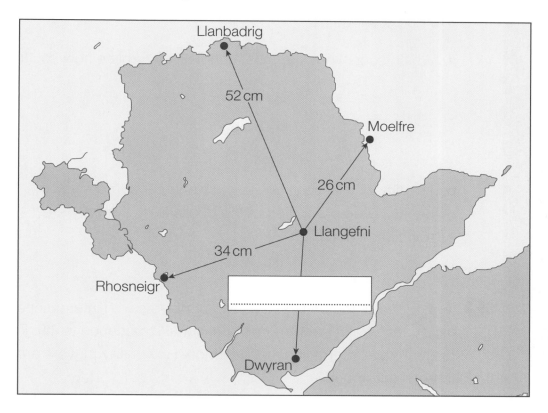

a. Complete this table to show the distance between these places. All journeys pass through Llangefni. **(2 marks)**

	Rhosneigr	Llanbadrig	Moelfre	Llangefni
Rhosneigr		....	....	....
Llanbadrig	....		....	26 km
Moelfre	....	....		....
Llangefni	....	26 km	....	

b. Dwyran is 42 km away from Llanbadrig. Complete the map to show the distance on the map from Llangefni to Dwyran in centimetres. **(1 mark)**

Solving problems

1 In the school library at John Street Primary School, three out of every seven books are non-fiction.

In the school library at nearby Ford Lane Academy, two out of every five books are non-fiction.

John Street's library has 595 books altogether. Ford Lane's library has 610 books altogether.

a. Which school has the most non-fiction? Explain how you know.

(2 marks)

....

....

b. The librarian at John Street buys another 85 non-fiction books. What proportion of the books in their library are non-fiction now? **(1 mark)**

....

2 In a squad of footballers, the ratio of players with international experience to those with no international experience is 2:9. Four players have international experience. How many players are there in the squad? **(1 mark)**

....

3 At a rugby match between England and Italy there are 82 000 spectators. The ratio of England to Italy supporters is 19:1. How many England supporters are there? **(1 mark)**

....

4 A bicycle costs £375. In a sale the price is reduced by 15 percent. What is the new price? **(1 mark)**

....

5 This is a plan of a nature area.

a. What percentage of the nature area is going to be the butterfly garden? **(1 mark)**

....

b. The pond is going to take up 20 percent of the area of the meadow.
What is the area of the pond? **(1 mark)**

....

6 Anesh normally buys 1.5 litre bottles of soft drink. At the supermarket he
notices a promotion bottle that has 25 percent extra. What is the capacity
of this new bottle? **(1 mark)**

....

7 Lily and Fay took a spelling test. The test was marked out of 20. Lily's test was
25 percent incorrect. Fay's test was 80 percent correct. How many more
answers did Fay get correct than Lily? **(1 mark)**

....

8 On a sketch map, the distance between Canterbury and Dover is 26 cm.
The scale of the map is 1:100 000.

a. How far is the actual distance between the two towns? **(1 mark)**

....

....

b. Another sketch map is at a scale of 1:25 000. How many centimetres would
there be between the two towns on this map? **(1 mark)**

....

....

Total $\frac{}{12}$

Missing numbers

1 **a.** $56 + \boxed{} = 100$ **(1 mark)**

b. $\boxed{} - 45 = 75$ **(1 mark)**

c. $134\,cm + \boxed{} = 2\,m$ **(1 mark)**

d. $\boxed{} - £4.32 = £5.68$ **(1 mark)**

e. $504 \div \boxed{} = 56$ **(1 mark)**

f. $\boxed{} \times 8 = 784$ **(1 mark)**

g. $£45.50 \div \boxed{} = £9.10$ **(1 mark)**

h. $\boxed{} \times 500\,m = 17\,km$ **(1 mark)**

2 Choose two numbers that will make these equations correct.

a. $8 \times \boxed{} = 24 \div \boxed{}$ **(1 mark)**

b. $7 \times \boxed{} = 60 - \boxed{}$ **(1 mark)**

3 Peter thinks of a number. He halves the number and then adds four. His answer is the same as the number he started with. What was Peter's number?   **(1 mark)**

....

4 ▲ = 6

▲ + ■ = ⬡

2 × ▲ = ⬡ − 2

What is the value of ■? ....   **(1 mark)**

Missing angles

1 Calculate the value of angle *w*.   **(1 mark)**

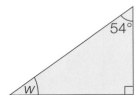

....

....

....

2 Calculate the value of angle y. **(1 mark)**

26°
y

Missing lengths

1 This shape is made from two regular hexagons and has a perimeter of 45 cm.
Calculate the length y. **(1 mark)**

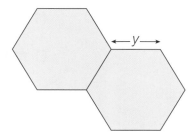
←y→

2 What is the value of l for this rectangle? **(1 mark)**

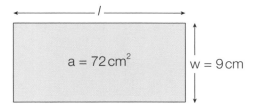
l
$a = 72\,\text{cm}^2$
$w = 9\,\text{cm}$

3 What is the value of h for this parallelogram? **(1 mark)**

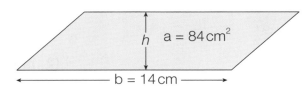
h
$a = 84\,\text{cm}^2$
$b = 14\,\text{cm}$

Total $\dfrac{}{17}$

Equations and expressions

1 What is the value of x when:

a. $x^2 + 4 = 20$? .... **(1 mark)**

b. $5x - 10 = 15$? .... **(1 mark)**

c. $50 - x = 35$? .... **(1 mark)**

d. $\dfrac{x}{9} = 7$? .... **(1 mark)**

2 If y is 6, what are the values of these expressions?

a. $\dfrac{2y + 8}{5}$ .... **(1 mark)**

b. $25y - 30$ .... **(1 mark)**

c. $4(y - 1) + 4(y + 1)$ .... **(1 mark)**

d. $2y^2 - 6$ .... **(1 mark)**

3 Find the missing numbers so that $6x + 2y = 50$

For example $6x + 2y = 50$ when $x = 6$ and $y = 7$

a. $6x + 2y = 50$ when $x = 5$ and $y = \boxed{}$ **(1 mark)**

b. $6x + 2y = 50$ when $x = \boxed{}$ and $y = 13$ **(1 mark)**

c. $6x + 2y = 50$ when $x = 3$ and $y = \boxed{}$ **(1 mark)**

4 Here are three equations.

$s = 2t$

$5t + u = 22$

$4u = 28$

What are the values of s, t and u?

$s = \boxed{}$ $t = \boxed{}$ $u = \boxed{}$ **(2 marks)**

Formulae

1 If a cuboid has length (*L*), width (*W*) and height (*H*), what is the formula that describes its volume (*V*)? **(1 mark)**

....

2 In a saltwater aquarium the formula to describe how many fish can be kept is:

$g = 3f$

f is every inch of fish in the aquarium.

g is the number of gallons of water.

a. Adele has three fish that measure 3 inches, 4 inches and 5 inches. How much water will she need in her aquarium? **(1 mark)**

....

b. Carmen has a 48-gallon aquarium. How many 2-inch-long fish can she keep in it? **(1 mark)**

....

3 The number of faces (*F*), edges (*E*) and vertices (*V*) in 3D shapes (polyhedra) can be described using the formula:

$E = F + V - 2$

Use this formula to complete the gaps in this table. **(2 marks)**

Shape	Number of edges (E)	Number of faces (F)	Number of vertices (V)
Octahedron	12	8	....
Dodecahedron	....	12	20
Icosahedron	30	....	12

Total 18

Number sequences

1 What are the next **three** numbers in each sequence?

a. 24, 32, 40, 48, ..., ..., ...   **(1 mark)**

b. −18, −15, −12, −9, ..., ..., ...   **(1 mark)**

c. 240, 120, 60, 30, ..., ..., ...   **(1 mark)**

d. 1.5, 7.5, 37.5, 187.5, ... , ... , ...   **(1 mark)**

e. 56, 47, 38, 29, ..., ..., ...   **(1 mark)**

f. 16, 12, 8, 4, ..., ..., ...   **(1 mark)**

Reasoning about number sequences

1 Seth says that 256 will be in this number sequence.

25, 50, 75, 100, 125....

Is he correct? Circle Yes or No.

Yes / No

Explain how you know.   **(1 mark)**

....

2 Halima makes a sequence of five numbers.

Her rule is to add the same amount each time.

Write in the missing numbers.   **(1 mark)**

6 ☐ ☐ ☐ 28

Pattern problems

1 A builder is laying a path using a line of regular pentagonal paving blocks.

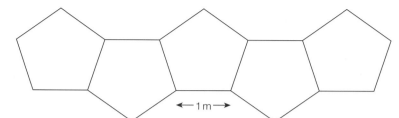

The number of paving blocks is *n*.

The perimeter of the path in metres is *p*.

a. Which expression describes the relationship between the number of
blocks and the perimeter in metres?
Tick one box. **(1 mark)**

$p = 5n$ ☐

$p = n + 5$ ☐

$p = 3n + 2$ ☐

$p = n^2$ ☐

b. The builder extends the path so that it contains 25 blocks.
What will the perimeter of the path be? **(1 mark)**

....

2 Akila is making a pattern from hexagons.

She says that to find the number of sides (*s*) you
need to multiply the number of hexagons (*n*) by
four and add two.

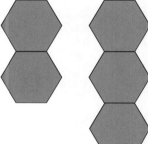

a. How many sides would a pattern of six
hexagons have? **(1 mark)**

....

b. Write Akila's rule as a formula. **(1 mark)**

....

Total $\frac{}{12}$

Length

1 **a.** Max is 152 cm tall. How tall is this in metres and centimetres?

.... **(1 mark)**

b. Meg runs 5.6 km in training. How far is this in metres?

.... **(1 mark)**

c. Mya's hand is 16 cm long. How long is it in millimetres?

.... **(1 mark)**

d. The rug on the hall floor is 0.75 m. How long is this in centimetres? .... **(1 mark)**

e. Mackenzie has 98 mm trimmed off his hair. How many centimetres is this? .... **(1 mark)**

2 Helena swims 24 lengths of a 25 m long pool. How far has she swum:

a. in metres? .... **(1 mark)**

b. in kilometres? .... **(1 mark)**

Mass and Weight

1 **a.** Baby Mae weighs 8000 g. How much is this in kilograms? .... **(1 mark)**

b. Willow uses 450 g of flour from a 1 kg bag. How many grams are left? .... **(1 mark)**

c. Gareth's guinea pig weighs 0.95 kg. How much is this in grams? .... **(1 mark)**

2 A packet of cereal holds 1.4 kg of cereal. It is divided into eight bowls. How many grams of cereal will be in each bowl?

.... **(1 mark)**

Capacity

1 **a.** How many millilitres are there in 70 cl of sparkling water?

.... **(1 mark)**

b. There are 1330 ml in a bottle of shampoo. What is this in litres?

.... **(1 mark)**

c. Express 0.8 litres as millilitres .... **(1 mark)**

2 Poppy opened a 1 litre carton of fruit juice and drank 450 ml.

How much was left? .... **(1 mark)**

Reading scales

1 **a.** Measure the amount of liquid in the cylinder. .... **(1 mark)**

b.

How many grams of flour are on the scales? .... **(1 mark)**

Total $\frac{}{17}$

Units of measurement

1 **a.** A film lasted 2 hours and 20 minutes. How long is this

in minutes? .... **(1 mark)**

b. Izumi swam four lengths in 21 seconds, 23 seconds, 22 seconds and 19 seconds. How long did it take him

altogether in minutes and seconds? .... **(1 mark)**

c. The running order for a dance show says 150 minutes.

How long is this in hours and minutes? .... **(1 mark)**

d. It takes $3\frac{1}{2}$ minutes to soft boil an egg. How long is this

in seconds? .... **(1 mark)**

Analogue and digital clocks

1 Draw lines to match the clock times to their digital equivalents.

(4 marks)

| twenty past seven | twenty to nine | ten past five | ten to four |

| 3.50 | 5.10 | 8.40 | 7.20 |

2 Write these as digital times.

a. twenty-five past six .... **(1 mark)**

b. quarter to nine .... **(1 mark)**

c. quarter past eleven .... **(1 mark)**

d. five past four .... **(1 mark)**

The 24 hour clock

1 Write these as 24 hr digital times.

a. ten past two in the morning .... **(1 mark)**

b. five to five in the afternoon .... **(1 mark)**

c. quarter past six in the evening .... **(1 mark)**

d. twenty five to seven in the morning .... **(1 mark)**

Time problems

1 The train to Buxton leaves Heaton Chapel at 8.57am and arrives in Buxton at 9.43am. How long is the journey? **(1 mark)**

....

....

2 The ferry to San Malo leaves Portsmouth at 8.50am. The journey is 9 hours and 20 minutes.
What time will it arrive in San Malo? **(1 mark)**

....

....

3 Here is a train timetable.

	Train 1	Train 2	Train 3
Stockport	09.15	10.20	11.20
Macclesfield	09.29	_____	11.32
Milton Keynes	10.45	12.00	_____
London	11.20	12.45	13.30

a. Which is the quickest train from Stockport to London? **(1 mark)**

....

b. Which is the slowest train from Stockport to London? **(1 mark)**

....

c. How long does the journey from Macclesfield to Milton Keynes take? **(1 mark)**

....

Total $\dfrac{}{21}$

Length

1 Work out:

    a. 5 inches = approximately .... cm   **(1 mark)**

    b. 10 inches = approximately .... cm   **(1 mark)**

    c. 1 foot = approximately .... cm   **(1 mark)**

    d. 3 feet 3 inches = approximately .... cm   **(1 mark)**

2 Ruben is 5 feet tall.
Approximately how tall is he in centimetres? .... cm   **(1 mark)**

3 Brooke's hair is 60 cm long.
Approximately how long is this in inches? .... inches   **(1 mark)**

Weight

1 Work out:

    a. 10 oz = approximately .... g   **(1 mark)**

    b. 2 lb = approximately .... g   **(1 mark)**

    c. 1 stone = approximately .... g   **(1 mark)**

2 A new baby weighs 8 lb.
Approximately how much is this in kilograms? .... kg   **(1 mark)**

3 A bag of potatoes weighs 5 kg.
Approximately how much is this in pounds? .... lb   **(1 mark)**

4 A cake recipe asks for 4 oz of sugar, 4 oz of flour and 4 oz of butter.

Approximately how much is this in grams? .... g   **(1 mark)**

Conversion graphs

1 Look at the graph and distance table (in kilometres) below.

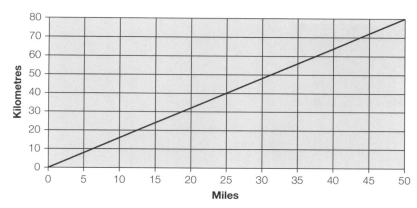

	Glastonbury	Yeovil	Exeter
Glastonbury	———	22 km	70 km
Yeovil	22 km	———	56 km
Exeter	70 km	56 km	———

a. What is the distance between Yeovil and Exeter:

   i. in kilometres? .... **(1 mark)**

  ii. in miles? .... **(1 mark)**

b. What is the distance of the journey from Glastonbury to Exeter in miles?

.... **(1 mark)**

c. What is the total distance of a trip from Glastonbury to Yeovil and back in miles?

.... **(1 mark)**

Total —— 16

Area of shapes

1 Calculate the area of the rectangle. **(1 mark)**

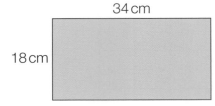

34 cm

18 cm

....

....

2 Calculate the area of the parallelogram. **(1 mark)**

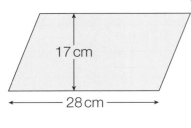

17 cm

28 cm

....

....

3 Calculate the area of the triangle. **(1 mark)**

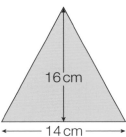

16 cm

14 cm

....

....

Compound shapes

1 Look at the compound shape below.

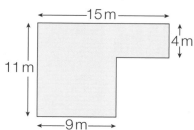

a. Calculate the perimeter of this compound shape. **(1 mark)**

....

b. Calculate the area of this compound shape. **(1 mark)**

....

....

Perimeter

1 Calculate the perimeter of this regular hexagon. **(1 mark)**

8 cm

....

2 Calculate the perimeter of this regular octagon. **(1 mark)**

6 cm

....

3 A regular pentagon has a perimeter of 45 cm. How long is each of its sides? **(1 mark)**

....

4 A regular heptagon has a perimeter of 56 cm. How long is each of its sides? **(1 mark)**

....

Total $\frac{}{9}$

Calculating volume

1 Calculate the volume of this cuboid. **(2 marks)**

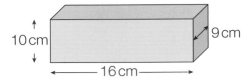

....

....

2 Calculate the volume of this cuboid. **(1 mark)**

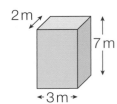

....

....

3 Calculate the volume of this cube. **(1 mark)**

....

....

Solving problems

1 Hannah has 36 one-centimetre cubes.
She uses all the cubes to build a cuboid 3 cm long by 3 cm wide.

a. How high is it? .... **(1 mark)**

b. Give the dimensions of another cuboid she could build
using all 36 cubes. **(1 mark)**

Length

Width

Height

2 Sid builds four raised beds in his garden. The dimensions of each bed are 2 m by 4 m. He wants to fill each one to a depth of 0.8 m of soil.

a. How much soil does he need? **(1 mark)**

....

b. The soil comes in 4 m³ bags. How many bags will he need to buy? **(1 mark)**

....

....

....

3 The owners of an aquatic life centre want to build a fish tank with a volume of 800 cubic metres.

What could the dimensions of the aquarium be? **(1 mark)**

	Length
	Width
	Height

4 A parcel has a volume of 504 cm³.
How long is it? **(1 mark)**

$h = 8\,cm$ $v = 504\,cm^3$ $w = 7\,cm$

....

....

5 A cuboid has two different faces.

| Area =
16 cm² | Area =
24 cm² |
| --- | --- |

What is the volume of the cuboid? **(1 mark)**

....

....

Total ——
11

Area

1 Measure the length and width of this rectangle.

Use these measurements to calculate the area .... **(1 mark)**

2 Measure the length and height of this parallelogram.

Use these measurements to calculate the area .... **(1 mark)**

Measuring angles

1 Use a protractor to measure these angles. **(2 marks)**

a.

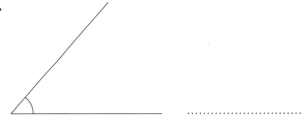

....

b.

....

Drawing shapes

1 Here is a drawing of a triangle.

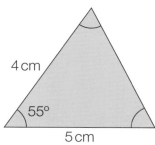

Draw the full-size triangle **accurately** in the box.
Use a protractor and a ruler.
Write in the length of the missing side and the size of the two missing angles.
One of the lines has been drawn for you.　**(2 marks)**

2 Here is a drawing of a quadrilateral.

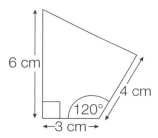

Draw the full-size quadrilateral **accurately** in the box.
Use a protractor and a ruler.
Write in the length of the missing side and the size of the two missing angles.
Two of the lines have been drawn for you.　**(2 marks)**

Total —— 8

2D shapes

1 Read the clues and write the **mathematical** name for this quadrilateral. **(1 mark)**

> It has four sides.
>
> It has two pairs of opposite parallel lines.
>
> It has two long sides the same length and two short sides the same length.
>
> It does not have any right angles.

....

2 Read the clues and write the **mathematical** name for this quadrilateral. **(1 mark)**

> It has four sides.
>
> It has two pairs of opposite parallel lines.
>
> It has two long sides the same length.
>
> It has two short sides the same length.
>
> It has four right angles.

....

3 Read the clues and write the **mathematical** name for this quadrilateral. **(1 mark)**

> It has four sides.
>
> It has two pairs of adjacent sides that are equal in length.

....

Triangles

1 Draw a line to match each triangle to its definition. **(2 marks)**

scalene	isosceles	equilateral	right-angled

one right-angle of 90°	two equal sides and two equal angles	no equal sides or angles	all sides and angles are equal

3D shapes

1 Identify each shape from its net.

a.

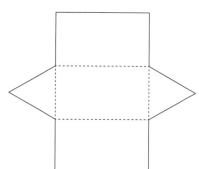

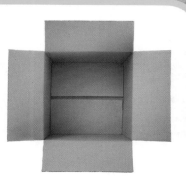

.... **(1 mark)**

b.

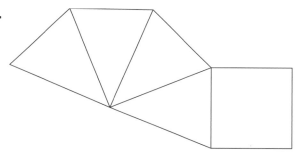

.... **(1 mark)**

2

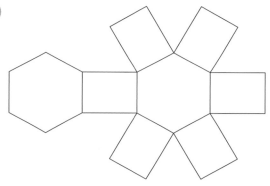

a. What 3D shape is this a net for? .... **(1 mark)**

b. How many faces, edges and vertices does it have? .... **(1 mark)**

3 Freddie has these shapes.

The pyramid can sit exactly on top of the cube to make a new shape.
How many faces does this new shape have? **(1 mark)**

....

Total — 10

Circles and turns

1 The radius of a circle is 12 cm.

a. What is its diameter? ....   **(1 mark)**

b. What is its circumference? ....   **(1 mark)**

> Remember: the circumference of a circle is **3.14 × diameter**.

2 The diameter of a circle is 44 cm.

a. What is its radius? ....   **(1 mark)**

b. What is its circumference? ....   **(1 mark)**

3 **a.** What is the value of a quarter turn

around a circle, in degrees? ....   **(1 mark)**

b. What is the value of a three-quarter turn

around a circle, in degrees? ....   **(1 mark)**

Angles in triangles

1 **a.** What is the value of angle z? ....   **(1 mark)**

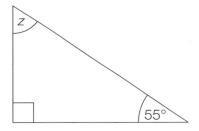

b. **i.** What is the value of angle a? ....   **(1 mark)**

ii. What is the value of angle b? ....   **(1 mark)**

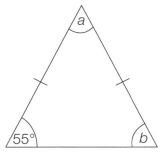

Calculating angles

1 Calculate the value of *x* .... **(1 mark)**

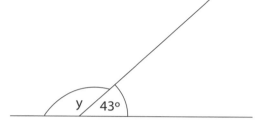

125°

x

2 Calculate the value of *y* .... **(1 mark)**

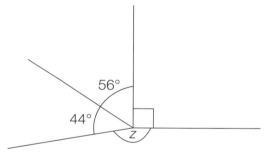

y / 43°

3 Calculate the value of *z* .... **(1 mark)**

56°

44°

z

4 Calculate the values of angles *a* and *b*.

102°

a

b

a = ... *b* = ... **(2 marks)**

Coordinates

❶ Look at this grid with four quadrants.

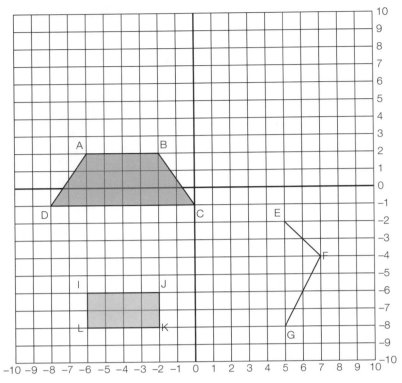

a. On the grid plot the parallelogram with corners (−5, 9), (2, 9), (4, 4) and (−3, 4).   **(1 mark)**

b. Write the coordinates of the corners of trapezium ABCD.   **(1 mark)**

....

c. Lines EF and FG are two sides of the kite EFGH. Using a ruler, complete the kite and give the coordinates of corner H.   **(1 mark)**

....

d. Rectangle IJKL has an area of eight squares.
Using a ruler, draw a similar rectangle that has four times the area of IJKL but has the same centre, (−4, −7).
What are the coordinates of the corners of this new rectangle?
(1 mark)

....

2 Look at isosceles triangle ABC. What are the coordinates of corner A? **(1 mark)**

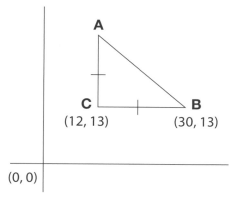

A

C
(12, 13)

B
(30, 13)

(0, 0)

Reflections and translations

1 Reflect the kite ABCD in the mirror line $x = y$. **(1 mark)**

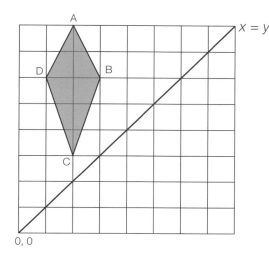

A

$x = y$

D

B

C

0, 0

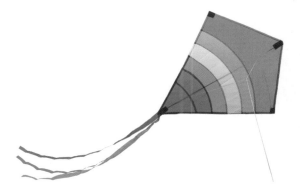

2 Translate the trapezium EFGH so that the (x, y) coordinates become $(x + 2, y - 3)$. **(1 mark)**

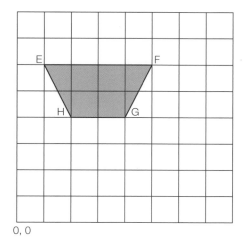

E

F

H

G

0, 0

Remember to use the correct words when describing direction, e.g. walk **along** the corridor before you go **up** (or **down**) the stairs.

Top tip!

Total $\frac{}{7}$

Understanding pie charts

❶ On a school residential trip, 64 children choose a sandwich filling. Twice as many children chose egg as ham. This pie chart shows the results.

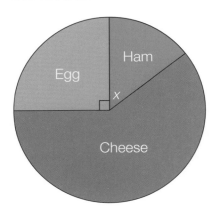

a. What is the value of angle x?   **(1 mark)**

....

b. How many children chose cheese?   **(1 mark)**

....

c. What percentage of children chose egg?   **(1 mark)**

....

❷ Beth and Shelley are counting the species of tree in two different woods. They display their results as pie charts.

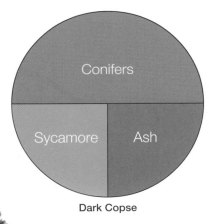

Dark Copse

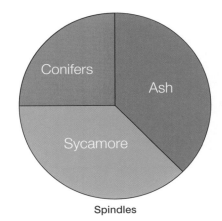

Spindles

In both woods there were equal numbers of Ash and Sycamore trees.
At Dark Copse they counted 44 conifer trees.
At Spindles they counted 40 conifer trees.

How many more Ash trees were there at Spindles than at Dark Copse?   **(2 marks)**

....

....

....

Drawing pie charts

1 Twenty-four children in Class 6 were asked what their favourite milkshake was. The results are shown below.

Strawberry	Banana	Chocolate	Vanilla	Total
5	2	10	7	24

Using a pencil, ruler and protractor, construct a pie chart that shows this information.   **(3 marks)**

Line graphs

❶ This line graph shows the average daytime temperature in London throughout the year.

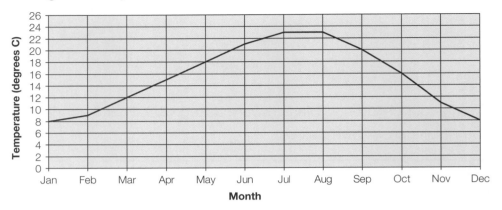

a. What is the difference between the highest and lowest monthly averages? **(1 mark)**

....

b. How much warmer is it in June than in April? **(1 mark)**

....

❷ Imogen is going on Holiday to Turkey. The currency in Turkey is the Turkish Lira. She prints a conversion graph to take with her.

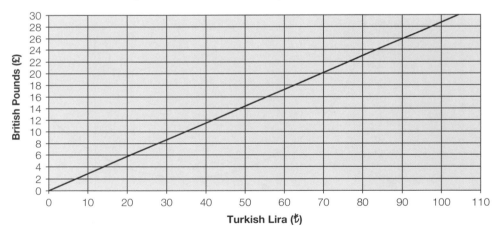

a. Imogen is allowed to take £25 pocket money. Approximately how many Lira will this be equivalent to? **(1 mark)**

....

b. On the first day she spends 20 Lira on a snack. Approximately how much is this in pounds? **(1 mark)**

....

c. Before leaving she spends 55 Lira on souvenirs. Approximately how much is this in pounds? **(1 mark)**

....

d. When she returns to the UK she exchanges all her remaining Lira for pounds and receives £9.00. Approximately how many Lira did she exchange? **(1 mark)**

....

Averages

1 Calculate the arithmetic average (mean) of these sets of numbers.

a. 4, 5, 5, 5, 6, **(1 mark)**

....

b. 246, 250, 251, 256, 257 **(1 mark)**

....

c. £16.40, £18.30, £24.40, £25.30 **(1 mark)**

....

d. 1, 1, 1.2, 1.4, 1.9, 2.5 **(1 mark)**

....

2 Fifteen children compared their shoe sizes. They wrote their findings as a list.

3, 3, 3½, 4, 4, 4, 4, 4½, 5, 5, 5½, 5½, 6, 6, 6

a. What is the average (median) shoe size? **(1 mark)**

....

b. What is the average (mode) shoe size? **(1 mark)**

....

3 Raúl rolled a dice four times and recorded his scores: 4, 3, 2 and 6.
He rolled the dice a fifth time and then calculated the average (mean) score to be 4.
What was his fifth dice roll? **(1 mark)**

....

Total $\frac{}{13}$

1 Here is a table of some temperatures around the world.

City	Temperature in °C
Aberdeen	−2°
Lima	17°
Oslo	−6°
Moscow	−8°
Madrid	21°

   a. What is the difference in temperature between Aberdeen and Madrid? **(1 mark)**

   b. What is the biggest temperature difference? **(1 mark)**

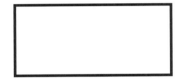

2 (Circle) the number that is closest in value to 0.6 **(1 mark)**

   0.06   0.59   0.65   0.8   0.5

3 Write these numbers in order, starting with the smallest. **(1 mark)**

   7.17   1.7   7.119   7.2   1.78

4 Which is the largest fraction: $\frac{4}{8}$ or $\frac{10}{16}$? **(2 marks)**

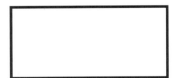

5 Tick the **two** fractions that are equivalent. **(1 mark)**

   $\frac{3}{4}$ ☐ $\frac{6}{10}$ ☐ $\frac{9}{12}$ ☐ $\frac{18}{20}$ ☐ $\frac{6}{7}$ ☐

6 Calculate 20% of 4800. **(1 mark)**

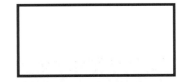

7 20 percent of George's football cards is 36 cards.

What is 50 percent? **(1 mark)**

8 A sequence of numbers increases by 60 every time.

60   120   180   240   300   360   ....

a. What are the next three numbers in the sequence? **(1 mark)**

b. Will 720 be in the sequence?
Circle Yes or No.

Yes / No **(1 mark)**

Explain how you know. **(1 mark)**

....

....

9 Ayesha made a sequence of five numbers.
The first number is four.
The last number is 24.

She added the **same amount** each time. Write in the
missing numbers. **(1 mark)**

4   24

⑩

34567 + 5792 =

1 mark

⑪ Samira has £12.50.

She buys a DVD for £5.79 and a bag for £4.25.

How much money will she have left?　　　　　　　　　　　**(1 mark)**

⑫ Put in the missing numbers to complete these calculations.

a. 687 –  = 432　　　　　　　　**(1 mark)**

b.  – 349 = 236　　　　　　　　**(1 mark)**

⑬ An aeroplane takes off with 758 passengers on board.

316 get off in Dubai.

A further 78 get off in Sri Lanka.

How many passengers are left when the plane arrives in Thailand?　**(1 mark)**

14

732 × 34 =

1 mark

15 Eva buys 12 sheets of stamps at the Post Office. Each sheet has 18 rows of stamps with 24 stamps in each row.

How many stamps are there altogether?

(1 mark)

16

946 ÷ 32 =

1 mark

17 Look at these equations.

$x = 2y$

$y = 3z$

Which equation below is also true?

Circle the correct one.

(1 mark)

$y = 2x$ $\qquad$ $x = 6y$ $\qquad$ $2z = x$ $\qquad$ $x = 6z$

18 Bushra buys a dozen bottles of sparkling water for £8.40.

How much does one bottle cost?

(1 mark)

19 Pilar's family are travelling by car from Manchester to Madrid. As well as a ferry crossing, they must drive 2072 km.

Pilar knows that 8 km is about the same distance as 5 miles.

How many miles must they drive?

(1 mark)

20 Florence buys a t-shirt to fit chest size 28 inches.

1 inch is approximately 2.5 cm.

What is the chest size in centimetres?

(1 mark)

21

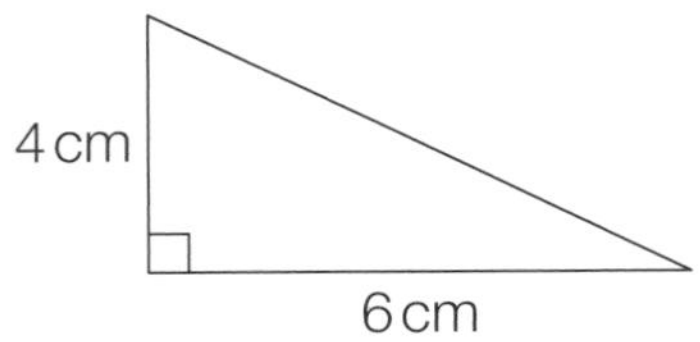

4 cm

6 cm

Draw the full size triangle accurately in the box below.

Use a ruler, protractor and set square.

(1 mark)

22 Sixty children were asked to choose their favourite flavour of ice-cream.

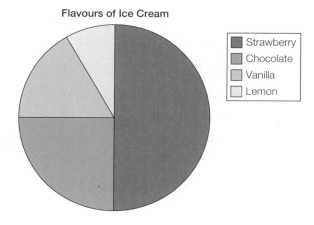

Flavours of Ice Cream

- Strawberry
- Chocolate
- Vanilla
- Lemon

Five children chose lemon.

a. How many children chose vanilla?

(1 mark)

b. What percentage of children chose chocolate?

(1 mark)

23 The base of the box is 15 cm by 8 cm. The height is 10 cm.

10 cm

←——15 cm——→ 8 cm

What is the volume of the box?

(1 mark)

24 An ice-skating rink is 25.5 m long and 15.5 m wide.
What is its perimeter?

(1 mark)

Acute – Any angle less than 90°

Addition – Joining several numbers together to find their total.

Adjacent – Adjacent lines are next to each other.

Algebra – Maths where numbers or values are represented by letters or symbols.

Angle – The amount of turn between two straight lines that are joined at a point.

Area – The size that a surface takes up measured in 'square' **units of measurement**, for example square metres (m²).

Arithmetic sequence – A sequence that increases or decreases by the same amount each time.

Capacity – The amount of liquid that a container can hold.

Common denominator – When working with fractions with different denominators, convert them to equivalent fractions with the same or common denominator. This number should be a multiple of both denominators.

Common difference – The value in a sequence that each term increases or decreases by.

Continuous data – Data that has any value within a certain range, for example the temperature throughout the day.

Coordinates – Pairs of numbers that show the exact position of a point on a grid. Normally within brackets and separated by a comma.

Data – A collection of information which might be numbers, facts or measurements. Data is often organised into tables and displayed as charts or graphs to make it easier to understand.

Decimal fraction – Any fraction where the denominator is a power of 10, for example 10, 100 or 1000. Writing a fraction with a decimal point instead of a denominator makes it easier to complete operations. Often just called decimals.

Decimal places – Decides how accurate a decimal answer is. For example a decimal rounded to one decimal place will be rounded to the nearest tenth. 3.78 → 3.8

Decimal point – Dot used to separate the decimal fraction from the whole part of a number.

Decreasing – Making an amount smaller.

Digit – Every individual figure in a number is a digit.

Digital sum – To find the digital sum of a number keep on adding the digits together until you get to a single digit number. For example the digital sum of 909 is 9 so you know that it is a multiple of 9. (9 + 0 + 9 = 18, 1 + 8 = 9)

Discrete data – Can only take certain values. For example days of the week or shoe sizes.

Division – The **inverse** of multiplication. Either think of sharing an amount equally, for example 25 sweets shared between 5 friends equals 5 sweets each, or grouping objects, for example how many half-dozen egg boxes are needed to hold 36 eggs? 6 groups of 6 equal 36.

Divisor – The amount that you are dividing by. It might be a whole number, a fraction or a decimal.

Equation – An equation uses an equals sign to separate two expressions with the same value, for example $2x = 10$ or $5 \times 3 = 10 + 5$.

Equivalent fractions – Different fractions that represent the same amount.

Estimating – Making a rough or approximate calculation to help you solve a problem.

Expression – Numbers, symbols and operation signs ($\times$, $\div$, $+$ and $-$) grouped together to show the value of something, for example $2 + 3$ or $7y + 3$.

Factor – A whole number that divides exactly into another whole number. For example both 6 and 8 are factors of 48 because they divide into 48 without leaving a remainder.

FDP – Fraction, decimal and percentage. Three different ways of showing the same part of a quantity, total or size.

Formula – Formulae are rules that show the relationship between different **variables** in maths and science. They are usually written as **equations**.

Fraction – Any part of a number, part or whole. For example, $\frac{3}{4}$ means 3 out of 4 equal parts. The top number is the numerator and the bottom number is the denominator.

Fractions of an amount – If you divide a quantity, total or size into equal parts then these are fractions of that amount. For example a quarter of a metre is 25 cm. $\frac{1}{4}$ of 100 cm = 25 cm.

Geometric sequence – A sequence that changes by multiplying by some value.

Improper fractions – Any fraction where the **numerator** is bigger than the denominator. They are "top-heavy" fractions, for example $\frac{10}{8}$.

Increasing – Making an amount larger.

Integer – Also called whole numbers, integers can be positive or negative but not fractions or decimal numbers.

Inverse – The inverse or opposite operation can be used to check your answer. So you could check a subtraction answer by doing an addition or a division answer by doing a multiplication.

Isosceles – A triangle with two equal sides and two equal angles.

Mass – The amount of matter an object consists of. Your mass would be the same on Earth or in space.

Mean – Also called the arithmetic average. Add up all the values and divide by the number of values to find the mean.

Median – The middle value when all the values in a set of data are arranged from smallest to largest.

Metric measures – A decimal system of measurement that uses multiples of 10.

Mixed numbers – Numbers that are a mix of integer and fraction, for example $4\frac{3}{5}$.

Mode – The most commonly occurring value in a set of values.

Multiple – If a number divides by another without leaving a remainder then it's a multiple of that number. For example 48 is a multiple of both 6 and 8 because $48 \div 6 = 8$.

Multiplying – A short way to add the same number together many times, you might hear this called 'lots of'. You will need to know the multiplication tables.

Negative numbers – Numbers less than zero.

Non-unit fractions – Any fraction with a numerator greater than one.

Obtuse – Any angle between 90° and 180°

Operation – Grown-ups may know these as sums. They could be addition, subtraction, multiplication or division. Operations might also be things like squaring a number.

Parallel – Parallel lines always stay the same distance apart and never meet.

Partition – Breaking up a number into its separate parts, for example hundreds, tens and ones, to help you complete operations like multiplication.

Percentage – A percentage is a fraction out of 100 and is usually shown using the % symbol.

Perimeter – The distance around the outside of a shape. The perimeter of a circle is called the circumference.

Perpendicular – Perpendicular lines are at a right angle (90°) to each other.

Pie chart – A special chart that shows the relative sizes of data as sectors of a circle.

Place value – The position or place of each digit decides what value it has in the number.

Polygon – Any 2D shape with three or more straight sides.

Polyhedron – A 3D shape with flat faces.

Prime number – A whole number that has exactly two factors, one and itself. For example 7 only has factors 1 and 7. 1 doesn't qualify because it only has one factor!

Proportion – A part of an amount compared to the whole. For example the proportion of white cars is one in every five. You can write this as a fraction, $\frac{1}{5}$.

Quadrant – The four areas that are created when you divide a grid with an x and a y axis.

Ratio – Compares different parts of the whole amount to each other. For example the ratio of red to white cars is three to four. You can write this as a ratio, 3:4.

Reasoning – Explaining and justifying your answer, for example by showing how you know that something is correct.

Recurring decimal – Decimals that have a repeating digit or a repeating pattern of digits. You might round them to a number of decimal places or use a symbol to show that they recur. For example $\frac{1}{3}$ can be shown as $0.\dot{3}$

Reduce – Simplify a fraction to get the lowest numerator and denominator possible.

Reflection – A shape that is reflected is flipped across a mirror line without changing its size.

Reflex – Any angle between 180° and 360°

Regular – A polygon with all sides and all angles the same size.

Remainder – What's left over when the number you are dividing is not a multiple of the divisor. You can write it as a whole number (**integer**), fraction or decimal. In problems you usually have to round your remainder either up or down.

Rounding – Changing a number to a more convenient value, for example the nearest ten, hundred or thousand.

Scale factor – A ratio that expresses the amount of enlargement or a ratio between two sets of measurements.

Scale – If you scale something you reduce or enlarge all of its dimensions.

The scale of a map or drawing refers to the ratio between the measurements on the model or drawing and the size of the actual object or distance.
A scale can also be a set of marks on a measuring instrument.

Sequence – An ordered set of numbers shapes or objects arranged according to a rule.

Similar – Shapes that are similar are the same shape as each other but not necessarily the same size.

Simplify – Divide both numbers in a fraction, ratio or proportion by the same number to make them easier to understand.

Square – To find the square of a whole number you simply multiply it by itself. For example $4 \times 4 = 16$. You can show that a number is squared with a symbol $9^2 = 81$.

Square root – The opposite of squaring. So the square root of 25 is 5. This is usually shown with a symbol, $\sqrt{\ }$. You can find this symbol on a calculator.

Straight angle – An angle that is exactly 180°

Subtracting – Taking one number away from another. You might hear it called 'the difference between', minus or simply taking-away.

Term – One of the numbers in a sequence

Translation – To move or 'slide' a shape to a new position on a grid without changing its size or appearance.

Unit fractions – Any fraction with a numerator of one.

Units of measurement – Most mathematics in real life involves money or measures. When giving an answer to a problem, remember to include the correct units of measurement, for example euros (€) or square metres (m^2).

Variable – A value in an equation that is represented by a symbol or letter.

Volume – The volume is the amount of space taken up by a three dimensional (3D) object. It is measured in cubic units, for example cubic centimetres (cm^3)

Weight – The **mass** of an object multiplied by gravity.